What About Grace?

By Arthur Bailey

What About Grace?

Arthur Bailey
Arthur Bailey Ministries
PO Box 49744
Charlotte, NC 28277

Published and produced in the United States of America
ISBN: 978-15174817-1-1
Library of Congress Control Number: 2015953020
Edited by Higher Heart Productions

©MMXV Arthur Bailey Ministries. All Rights Reserved. No part of this book may be reproduced, shared, or transmitted by any means whether electronic, mechanical, photographic (including photocopy), recording, or otherwise without written permission from the author.

For more information visit www.ArthurBaileyMinistries.com

Text is 12 point Calibri and Times New Roman

This booklet is designed to accompany the Arthur Bailey Ministries video teachings by the same title.

Table of Contents

Chapter One 4

Chapter Two 33

Chapter Three 63

   Luther and the Law 86

   Luther and Anti-Semitism 89

Chapter Four 97

   Luther and Faith Alone 106

Chapter Five 123

DVD Teachings by Arthur Bailey 157

Chapter One

Today we are going to be embarking on a new venture. We've heard a whole lot about "grace" and "greasy grace" and grace as far as salvation goes and what all of that means. I've been compelled with all of the conversations, to tackle this.

Every time we get into the Feasts and with all of the conversations that I've had with individuals concerning the Sabbath, we always end up on the subject of "grace" and "What About Grace." I've asked several of you to present topics that you would like for us to discuss. This particular topic came up more than once.

I felt compelled here in the last few days to deal with this topic. I'm going to try to do an in-depth study on this whole idea of grace. Today we'll be doing the introduction of "What About Grace?" and lay a foundation.

The way that many people talk about grace, it appears to them that grace is a New Testament concept. The fact of the matter is that we are going to find out that even from the New Testament, the grace that is being referred to is not a New Testament concept, but an Old Testament concept. We're probably going to step on some toes and tip over some sacred cows and everything in between.

Like many recent teachings here, I've had to pull myself away from the preparation so that I can prepare the teaching. The preparation in itself has been so eye-opening for me on a number of levels.

As I present this, I want to do it in such a way that I'm not trying to tickle your ears or enlarge your head. I want to present it in such a way that *you* can present it. That's the goal; to equip you to minister to those people who always want to go into default mode once you have cornered them on every other question. They are going into a default mode.

"Well, what about grace?"

We're going to go into the default mode answer. Hopefully you'll be a lot more equipped to minister to other people who want to simply focus on the "grace" side of the Kingdom in the gospel. This is the topic.

"What about grace?"

Yes, it is with a question mark that we are going to be dealing with this topic. We're going to be looking at this subject of grace and we're going to go through the Bible. As I've shared with you in times past, having the advantage of going through various denominations and not only just being in a denomination, but being trained; there is a difference. There are a lot of us who have been part of denominations.

What I've found is that in many of the denominations, many of the people who are part of the denominations don't even really know the doctrinal beliefs of the organization that they serve or that they are serving in.

I've been with people. I've talked with people who are Jesus-only people. There are people who are in the Apostolic faith; the Holiness or the Ultra-Orthodox faith. They know that they baptize in Jesus' name. They know everybody prays in Jesus' name. They know everything they do in Jesus' name and yet they don't even know that they are "Jesus-only." They don't even know what that means; but the people in the denominations know what that means.

A person who is looking for a church home is not necessarily looking into what that church actually believes as much as they are looking for a place where they can have fellowship with other so-called like-minded people. Because their conversations are so on the surface, many people don't get to know in-depth the like-minded people that they are supposedly in fellowship with. When they begin to go in-depth in the relationship, they realize that they may not be as like-minded as they thought they were.

About this whole concept of grace; we're going to see where it actually came from. What I mean by the concept of grace is that I am talking about how grace is defined by modern-day religion. We're going to look at how grace is defined in the Bible. Then we are going to compare it to how it is defined by modern-day religion. You are going to see that there is a distinction in the definition.

We're going to look at the actual foundation of this philosophy. Then we're going to go in a variety of directions. I'm going to try to put it all into a nice, neat package. I have to give it to you in such a way that you can remember it; but also to understand it and then be able to articulate it. In case you don't understand it, we've got the video in the archives. Therefore you will always be able to go back and study and search and research. Amen?

As I've shared with you in the past and just as many have seen within the Bible, every Bible translation has its own instructions. Typically you find these in the front of the book.

Notice what most television preachers do. They hold the Bible in their hand, but they hardly ever read from it. They just want you to see it. Do you hear what I'm saying? They'll hold it and they'll talk about it. Then they'll put their screen up and you'll see the scripture references.

There's only one person that I know – actually two out there that I know of, who actually turn the pages. You will notice that many of them never leave from the front page because they've got all of their notes right there. They'll close it and open it and all of their notes are right there; but you don't see that.

People think that they are reading from the Bible, but they are actually reading from their notes. You begin to see all of the tricks. This is the stuff that you learn when you are in the denominations and are going through the training to do the presentations of teachings. So I'm sitting back and I'm watching preachers preach and I'm looking at all of their tricks. I said this to somebody else and they said to me:

"You know, I don't look at TV like that!"

Most people don't. People don't analyze what they see. They just watch and swallow. Often times they just swallow. They eat and swallow; hook, line and sinker. They believe that just because somebody has a Bible in their hands and they are reading from it, that it must be the word of God. I mean it really gets to a point where when you start debating with someone and they are debating from the notes on the side; the commentary on the side, it's like:

> "You do know that just because that is in your Bible, that it is not Bible."

Think about it. If somebody holds this book up and says:

> "I believe in this book – the word of God, the unadulterated word of God from the front of the book to the back of the book; from *Genesis* to *Revelation*..."

If you open the book and in the book there is all of this commentary from *Genesis* to *Revelation*, what you've just confessed if you have one of those books, is that you believe in *everything* that is in the book. So now the commentary becomes "Bible."

I'm telling you that people write their own Bibles basically for two reasons. One is for money because they can sell it and can make money. But two is to put their notes in it so that they have done your study for you. If you have a question about any doctrinal belief or anything that their church believes, they've got the answer in that Bible and that is what you read.

We're going to look at the actual scriptures. I broke this one down because there are a lot of key words. I think of all of the denominations that I've been in. I've been in the Baptist, I've been in the Pentecostal and the Charismatic and the Missouri Synod Lutheran and the Christian Reformed Church of North America; the Independents and of course studying in Messianic Judaism.

What I've come to find is that out of all of the denominations that I have been in and have had to go through their training, the ones that seemed to be the most serious about Bible training have been the Baptists. They are more serious than the Pentecostals. All they want to do is to speak in tongues. They get the Holy Ghost. That's all they need; the Holy Ghost and Jesus. Do you understand?

The denominations like the Missouri Synod Lutherans and the Reformed are more concerned about maintaining their culture within the confines of the book. We're going to look at some of that because often times people don't know that a lot of the doctrines that we have come from a cultural perspective other than from the book. So we're going to look at that.

Turn with me if you would to *Ephesians* chapter two. When you see what I've done to this verse; when I first started studying with the Baptists, they encouraged me to get a Key Word Study Bible. The Key Word Study Bible would look something like this (holds up book) except that where you see the bold letters and the underlined letters, you would see a Strong's number by it.

That Strong's number is saying here are the key words in this particular verse, or at least here are the words that we think are key in this particular verse. In order for you to understand this verse as we are trying to communicate it, you need to look up these key words. And here is the Strong's numbering system so that you don't have to spend a whole lot of time. You've got the numbers, go look up the numbers. Those will help you to understand this verse.

If you have a Key Word Study Bible with you today and it has the Hebrew and the Greek key words, you will find that you've got some words underlined in bold that are not underlined in bold in the Key Word Study Bible. The reason for that is because for the most part when people read *Ephesians* 2:8, here is what they hear:

> Eph 2:8-9 – "For by **grace** are ye **saved** through **faith**; and that not of yourselves: *it*

> *is* the **gift** of God: ⁹Not of **works**, lest any man should **boast**."

When you look at the word "works," often times what people don't understand is that they are associating the language and the definition of their language to the words that they are reading. You see, if you are reading an English Bible, what are you going to associate definition-wise to the words that you read? It will be an English definition. That's normal.

If you were reading a Russian Bible, you wouldn't understand it. Now you have to get a *translation,* and unfortunately the Russian Bibles are [made] from the English translation. If you were reading an authentic Hebrew manuscript or an authentic Greek manuscript and you are an English-speaking person, you would be forced to look this up in the Hebrew and in the Greek in order to understand it. That is because you are dealing with a language and the definition of words that you have not learned.

So when you read the English version of the Bible, it is only logical that you are going to interpret the English version of the Bible with English words and the definition of words in the English language.

I took the liberty of pointing out what I think are the key words in this Bible or in this passage. One is "grace."

> Eph 2:8 – "For by grace are ye saved."

I need to know what "grace" is that saves me through faith. And now I need to understand "faith" because if I'm saved by grace through faith, then I need both grace and faith to be saved.

> "And that not of yourselves."

Okay, that's an interesting concept. That's not of myself, so what is it saying? It is saying that I can't save myself. The thing of it is that I can save myself on a human level, but I can't save myself on a spiritual level. You see, if I'm going through some trouble and I know how to fix the problem, then I've just saved myself. You say things like:

> "I just saved a bunch of money. I saved fifteen percent."

Do you know what I'm saying? You start thinking about savings, but you won't appropriate savings with this particular "save." You won't associate saving someone from falling off of a cliff or saving someone from bumping their head. Someone is about to fall and you save them. I mean there are a lot of ways that you can appropriate this "save." When you read it in the Bible, what do you think about? You think about being born again, going to heaven; not going to hell.

These are the typical terms that people associate with "save." What they do is when they get into a conversation that they don't really want to deal with, the question is:

> "Is it a salvation issue?"

Is it a salvation issue? If it is not a salvation issue; if it's not going to affect my salvation, then it's really not that detrimental. Now, if it is going to affect my salvation, then I need to learn about it. But if I am saved and I believe that "once I'm saved I'm always saved," then nothing can affect my salvation. So nothing you say matters because I'm "saved."

Here I need grace and faith, but typically it is like the Young Men's Christian Association. The Young Men's Christian Association became the YMCA. And now what is it? It's the "Y." You see, over time individuals have a tendency to reduce the long wording to a letter, just like here.

The person who wants to argue "grace" says:

> "Listen brother, we're saved by grace — not through faith, but it's grace, and grace alone!"

Faith has nothing to do with it now. It has gone from *saved by grace through faith,* to *grace alone.* That's what humans do.

> "And that not of yourselves. It is the gift of God."

What is really interesting is that you would never think that you would have to look up the word "gift," because you associate gift as something that someone gives you without anything. You don't have to do anything, right? But do you know that if someone gives you a gift, you have to at least receive it?

> "Wait a minute. I don't have to receive it. I don't have to do anything for this gift!"

Oh, we're going to get heavy here folks.

> Eph 2:9 – "Not of works,"

What is "works," because I don't need it. Or do I? When I think of works in this particular passage, I appropriate or associate or define works through something that I am doing in order to obtain this free gift.

> "Not of works, lest any man should boast."

What is "boast" and why would any man boast? Have you ever boasted about being saved? Think about it. You see, Paul is saying some things here that people don't sometimes take the time to see exactly what he is saying, because they think they already know.

If you already think that you know the answer, then there is no point in searching it out. You don't look for answers you already have. You look for answers you don't have. The fact that we don't look for it is because we think we already know it. This is why we're having this conversation. This is why you are spending a lot of time talking to people who default to grace. You don't really have an effective way of communicating with them to show them. Even though you know it takes more than grace, you can't argue with grace – until now.

You have to ask yourself some questions. You always have to ask questions. When I approach this book, I don't see it as a leather-bound book. I don't see it as books with words. I see this book as the Almighty Himself. Now, I know that He is not the book, but think about the fact that Yeshua became flesh. He was the word that became flesh.

In order for me to know him, I have to know the word that he became; because he is the word. I can't know him apart from this book, because for lack of a better word, *he is the book that we call the word that became flesh*. You never see him reading from the book, because he *is* the book. So when the Pharisees came to him and said:

> "Where did you learn this stuff?"

He says:

> "Man, I AM. I'm the stuff you are reading about. I AM what you are reading. You just don't get it because you're looking to the scrolls. I'm the scroll. If you really want to know the scroll, you're looking at the scroll. I'm the talking scroll. I'm the walking scroll."

But they relied upon their book to argue with him and when they came at him from the book, the book schooled them. It shut them down. They didn't know what else to say. Guess what? He did it without the book. Why? Because he *is* the book.

When Paul wrote this passage in *Ephesians*, whom could Paul be referring to that could boast about their relationship to God in his day? I'm going to give you just a couple of seconds to answer that, because you already know.

Who would be boasting? Who would ever refer to themselves as being the "chosen people of God?" You see, if I already think I'm chosen by God, why do I need to be saved? It's the Jewish people.

> "We're the children of Abraham."

What does that mean? It means:

> "We're the covenant people."

Don't say that you're the children of Abraham. I can take some rocks and make them children of Abraham. You see, Paul is dealing with a people who already think that they are all right with Him. And when you already think that you are all right with Him, then you think that you are privileged.

> "We're not like those sinners. We're not like those Gentiles. We were born into this."

So Paul is not talking about Gentiles ladies and gentlemen, because Gentiles didn't go around boasting. They were worshipping idols. They weren't boasting. He says:

> Eph 2:8 - "For by grace are ye **saved** through **faith**; and that not of yourselves: *it is* the **gift** of God:"

Who is supposed to be serving God in Paul's day? There is only one group of people who were serving God. Everybody else was serving their god. Remember when you are looking at any writing of any book, you want to know who wrote it, to whom it was written, why it was written and the time that it was written in. If you can narrow that down, then you can do the research.

I don't have to do research about Paul in a time when Paul wasn't even born. So if I can kind of get a picture – I dare say that Paul wasn't one hundred years old. I can kind of do the research along the time that Paul existed; somewhere give or take 70 or 80 years.

I can take a look at the historical events that took place to verify places that Paul said that he was in – the historical archives, if there is such an archive. It is just like here in the United States of America and in any country. Any time any king is on the throne, that king has the archives and the chronicles of their kingdom.

These are the chronicles. Every king and every kingdom has scribes. So now here we are today. We can go back all the way into the kingdoms that existed during the time of Noah, because everything else before that is nonexistent as far as we know (except for the geography of it).

But here Paul is writing to a particular people. If you look at the book of *Acts* and you look at Paul's journeys, you will see who gave Paul problems. The ones who gave Paul problems; the ones who accused Paul of turning people away from the God of the Jews – you know who his problems are with. But people want to say:

"Paul had a problem with the Gentiles."

Paul didn't have a problem with the Gentiles until he started talking about their idols and witches or people who were making money and they began to lose money. Then of course he had a problem. But before that, the ones that Paul had a problem with; the ones who beat him, the ones who left him for dead, the ones who threw him in jail, the ones who chased him out of town, were religious people.

When you think about it, who would be working or earning their way to God's Heaven or afterlife in Paul's day? Who would it look like? Gentiles didn't even know who God was unless somebody went and told them. Keep in mind this fact, since all study material we have today is written by Christians or Jews. It is only natural that they would refer to the people of the book as Christians, Jews or Gentiles.

This irks me when I am reading first century material and they are writing in the first century that the people in the first century were Christians. Some even say that Jesus was a Christian! Do you understand what I am saying? How can there be Christians in the first century when the whole idea of "christos" is basically Greek and Latin?

Neither the Greek nor the Latin (speaking peoples) was even interested in the scriptures. The first translation of scripture was into Greek. It is called the *Septuagint,* and that wasn't done until a certain era. So how can you go back? And then the Septuagint was only the Old Testament.

The Old Testament was written in the language of Greek so that the Greek-speaking Jews could read the scriptures in their language. Do you understand what I am saying? There certainly weren't any Christians in the Torah!

Grace – what is it? *Charis* [khar′-ece]; that's the Greek word. It means "that which affords joy, pleasure, delight, sweetness, charm, loveliness: grace of speech; good will, loving-kindness, favour."

You hear people saying:

"How are you doing?"

"Well, I'm blessed and highly favored."

Basically what they are saying is that:

"I am blessed and highly graced."

Another definition is "of the merciful kindness by which God exerting his holy influence upon souls, turns them to Christ..."

I pointed that out because in all of this material that you are going to study from, you are going to see that they inject the word "Christ."

"...Keeps, strengthens, increases them in Christian faith..."

Really?

So during the time of Paul, Paul was writing to "Christians."

Really?

There was no such thing as a "Christian." They weren't called "Christians" at Antioch! In the English Bible they were. Do you get it?

> "They were first called Christians at Antioch."

There weren't any Christians at Antioch! The word had not even been invented yet. The idea of "Christians" didn't even come along until the Roman Catholics came onto the scene. There weren't any Roman Catholics in the book of *Acts,* but they interpreted the book of *Acts* from a Catholic perspective. Therefore they are associating modern words to the ancient scripture or the Bible.

So continuing the definition: "of merciful kindness by which God exerting his holy influence upon souls, turns them to Christ, keeps, strengthens, increases them in Christian faith, knowledge, affection and kindles them to the exercise of the Christian virtues."

It is like:

> "Man, really?"

You can tell this was written by a Christian. Now if it was a Jewish person writing it, they would probably say something else. It would be all Jewish, Jewish, Jewish. That's just like what you will find when someone who wants to teach will use the term "Jews" so loosely to the point where everybody who is of Israel is "Jewish."

One guy asked me:

"Do you love the Jewish people?"

I said:

"What Jewish people? Which ones?"

I can't say that I love the Jewish people when there may be some that I don't love. But you see, people want to put you into a blanket situation.

"Do you love Israel?"

You know, a guy said while I was in Israel:

"Do you love Israel?"

And I said:

"Which one? Which Israel are you talking about?"

Believe it or not, there are several. In the Bible, Jacob's name was changed to Israel. Second, there are the children of Israel. Third, there is the land of Israel. There are three "Israel's" right there, so the question is, which one? If you are going to tell me that "loving Israel" means loving the Jewish people, then I'm now going to have to tell you that I don't love all of the Jewish people.

Now there are Jews that I have met that I like and who have been nice and kind to me. Yes, I love them. But it's just like how I don't love all of the Black people or I don't love all of the Mexican people or I don't love all of the Asian people. How can I say that? I haven't met them all!

"Ooooh!"

Another grace definition is "what is due to grace, the spiritual condition of one governed by the power of divine grace; the token or proof of grace; benefit, a gift of grace, bounty, thanks, (for benefits, services, favours), recompense, reward."

All of these words are associated with grace. Here is how it is used. It is used 130 times — the word grace. This word *charis* is used six times as favour, four times as thanks, four times as thank and then pleasure. These are all the words that are associated with grace.

Whenever you see the word "grace" you have to look. Is it favor? Is it thanks? Is it pleasure or is it something else? Just because you read "grace" doesn't mean that every place that you read "grace" it is the same definition.

Saved – that's a good one, but what does it mean? There are a lot of words associated with it. The word *sozo* means "to save, to keep safe and sound and to rescue from danger or destruction."

You see, YeHoVaH *saved* the children of Israel in Egypt. He delivered them. He rescued them from danger. He rescued them from destruction. So in this particular sense, YeHoVaH was saving people throughout the Old Testament.

"But that's not what I mean by saved."

"Well, what do you mean?"

This is the kind of question we should ask. If I was to ask the average Messianic:

"Do you love the Jewish people?"

They will say:

"Yeah!"

But then I could say:

> "What about the ones who are going to come and burn your house down tomorrow? What about the ones who don't want you in the land?"

You see, you can't say that. You can say something like:

> "I love the people who love God."

How do I know that they love Him? I'm going to tell you something. There are a lot of Jewish people who hate God! They are atheists. They are anti-God. An atheist is simply a person who doesn't believe. There are some people who are "anti" and I will tell you this. The ones who are anti-the one He sent are the Anti-Messiahs! Don't get it twisted.

There are many Anti-Messiahs today. Those are the people who are against the Messiah and there are a lot of them who are Jewish. Now, I love them like God loves His world. Do you understand what I am saying? In that sense I love the entire world, because the earth is His; the fullness thereof and all they that dwell therein. So yes, I have that kind of love – the love of God who desires all men to be saved.

But do you know that if the people of Israel knew that I was coming over there to save them in the name of "Jesus" or in the name of "Yeshua," that they wouldn't even let me into the country?! So Yeshua weeps. YeHoVaH weeps and everybody is going to have to face judgment.

Definition of saved: "to keep safe and sound, rescue from danger or injury or peril."

Do you know that you can save a life by donating blood? You can save a life by giving a heart. You know, it won't be your life, but you can give a kidney. Do you know what I'm saying? You can save a life by donating an organ.

That's *salvation*. That person was going to die. You gave them an organ. That person lived. You just saved a life.

In the non-profit arena you have people who are asking you for money to save lives all of the time. They are not saving people as far as salvation is concerned. They are saving a person from going to bed hungry. They are saving a person from sleeping out in the cold. They are saving a person who needs insulin – if they don't get their insulin or if they don't get some food. They are in the saving business.

You can "save" someone and they can still go to hell. That is because there is *saving people* and then there is *saving grace*. There is grace and then there is the grace that saves. And this saving grace is the grace that comes from God that has appeared to all men. This grace requires something. There are a lot of graces that don't require anything.

You know that when you buy insurance, you have a grace period. From this time until this time after your premium is due, you have a period called grace. If you pay within that time period, then you are restored. You "saved" your insurance.

The definition continues: "to save a suffering one from perishing; (i.e. one suffering from disease, to make well, heal, restore to health)."

You will find that physicians believe that they are in the life-saving business. Paramedics believe that they are in the life-saving business. Do you understand what I am saying? So how do you distinguish the lives that they save from the lives that He saves? Is it the same salvation?

(Shakes head No.)

To them, they just saved a life. And to them they have committed their lives to saving lives. But you wouldn't associate the saving lives that they do to the saving of one's soul; although they will tell you that there have been a lot of souls coming through here. That is because they use the term soul loosely.

Definition: "to preserve one who is in danger of destruction; to save or rescue; to save in the technical biblical sense; negatively to deliver from the penalties of the Messianic judgment; to save from the evils which obstruct the reception of the Messianic deliverance."

The word is used ninety-three times as "to save," nine times as "to make whole," three times as "to heal," and two times as "to be whole." You will see that if you read that "your faith has made you whole," you may find the word *sozo* – saved.

When someone is healed, you will find that word. That's why you have to look it up. Sometimes you'll be surprised when you are looking up a word, that it is the same word that you will associate with something else.

Faith: We have looked at grace. We are saved by grace. We are saved by grace through what? Faith. That is this word *pistis*. It is Greek. It means: conviction of the truth of anything.

You see, when you are convicted of something, you have a choice. You can carry on as you have been, or change. If you change, you've done something. You've just changed. Why did you change? You changed because you heard the word of faith. Faith comes by hearing.

Once you've heard the word of faith and you recognize this word of faith as truth, this truth comes down inside of you and creates change. This now causes you to change your direction, to change your outlook, to change your position, to have a change of mind, or to do differently. This means that you are doing something based on the truth that has just come to you to help you free yourself from the destruction and the perilous path that you were on.

Definition: "conviction of the truth of anything, belief; in the New Testament of a conviction or belief respecting man's relationship to God and divine things, generally with the included idea of trust and holy fervour born of faith and joined with it; relating to God."

Also: "the conviction that God exists and is the creator and ruler of all things; the provider and bestower of eternal salvation through Messiah; relating to Messiah; a strong and welcome conviction or belief that Yeshua is the Messiah, through whom we obtain eternal salvation in the kingdom of God."

It is going to get interesting here in a minute.

Also: "the religious beliefs of Christians; belief with the predominant idea of trust (or confidence) whether in God or in Christ, springing from faith in the same; fidelity, faithfulness; the character of one who can be relied on."

One who has been in infidelity has violated what? The person that they have been unfaithful to. If you are a husband or a wife and your husband or wife has fallen into infidelity or walked into infidelity, they have violated your what?

Your trust – that is one of the views. They violated your trust. They violated your faith. You don't trust them. It is hard to put faith in them; whereas before you didn't have a problem trusting. You see, trusting is another word for faith; especially *pistis*.

Then there is this word "gift." Now this is interesting ladies and gentlemen, because you would probably never even think about looking up "gift" in the context of this passage. Gift is the Greek word *doron*, meaning: "a gift, present; gifts offered in expression of honour; of sacrifices and other gifts offered to God; of money cast into the treasury for the purposes of the temple and for the support of the poor; the offering of a gift or of gifts."

This word "gift" is used eighteen times in the Bible simply as that, a gift. But there is one time that the word is used as an offering. Do you know what is interesting? It is referring to:

> Hebrews 5:1 – "For every high priest taken from among men is ordained for men in things *pertaining* to God, that he may offer both gifts and sacrifices for sins:"

That word there is "offering." He became the sin offering.

Works *ergon,* meaning: "business." What is interesting is that we are not saved by works – not of works.

Employment: this is the key term for this idea of "works" in this word. "That which anyone is occupied; that which one undertakes to do; enterprise; undertaking; any product whatever, any thing accomplished by hand, art, industry or mind. Also: an act, deed."

It is interesting that there are people who believe that since the temple is no longer available, that their offerings are deeds; good deeds. This is why they have *sedaka* boxes. You've got Messianic congregations that have their little sedaka box and they have it in the back. People put their change and their coins in there. But do you know that there are sedaka boxes all over the land of Israel in virtually every place of business that we went in; even in the jewelry store?

They have these little cans where you can put the change in there. Here in America they've got these little things where you can put a quarter in or a dime or a nickel. You go into some places and you can put your loose change in there.

You see these things in Wal-Mart and other places and people get their change. They just put their change in there; Save a Child. You know, Make A Wish Foundation. There are balloons everywhere. In Israel they have boxes; sedaka boxes and they are for gifts of charity.

I'm watching people. You go into some places and you see religious Jews. They have a handful of change. They put some in that box, that box, that box, that box and that box. The folks on tours won't see stuff like that. You have to get in there where the people live.

Acts of charity: "good deeds" because good deeds are what keeps them "in favor with God." Are you seeing this? Good deeds: "acts of charity, acts of kindness."

So now on certain holidays or holy days, they go out and look for someone to whom they can do a good deed. That is because the good deed is what keeps them in good graces with the Almighty. The good deeds are them earning or continuing to earn the good graces.

So when Paul talks about how we are "saved by grace through faith," he is saying that we are not saved by grace through good deeds. It is not about works. Your deeds are not going to get you there. You need Messiah!

You have a person who is making long prayers. They are giving to the poor. They are doing acts of good deeds for people on special days. This causes them to be in "right standing" with the Almighty. Paul comes along and says:

> "Look guys, that isn't going to work. Your acts of kindness and your good deeds and all of the things that you are doing are not going to get you there."

You can swing chickens on *Yom Kippur* and you can do all of these things. You can try to get the temple rebuilt. People are at the wall wailing and waiting for the temple to be rebuilt so they can go back to the sacrificial system and so they can please God through sacrifices. But until they can please God through sacrifices, they are going to do all of these good deeds to try to keep the favor of God.

It is really amazing because you see, people want to say:

> "Well, that's nothing but the hand of God."

It's like, do you know what? If you are going to attribute these acts as nothing but the hand of God, then how can you not attribute the same acts to people over there that have nothing to do with God? But you will say:

"Well, God didn't save them."

How is it that terrorists can go in and take cities and bomb and build and rebuild? You see ladies and gentlemen, what people have a hard time figuring out sometimes is this. We read in the book of *Revelation* and we talk about the seven churches of Asia Minor – the seven churches of Asia Minor which the hand of God was supposed to be on, but He had warned them. None of them exist today – none of them. Those entire places have been taken over by Muslims. How did God "allow" that to happen? Is God with the Muslims and not with the Christians?

Do you understand what I am saying? Sometimes only a part of our brain works when it comes to Israel. We don't apply the same principles when it comes down to other parts of the world. Many have already come to the conclusion that those are God's chosen people, when the fact of it is that *the only ones who can come to God have to come through Messiah.*

How can anybody even go to him? You see, this is where the tricky theology comes in. You have people who are preaching Yeshua, but who believe that there is a group of people who don't need Yeshua to see the favor and blessings of YeHoVaH on their lives! At the same time they are rejecting the Yeshua that you are preaching! So does the Almighty have a double standard?

If you can come to that conclusion, you can say that there is a Sabbath for the Christians and a Sabbath for the Jews. You would say that the Jews have to keep the Law because that's what keeps them in good grace with God. But the Christians don't have to keep the Law because they've got Jesus and that is what keeps them in good grace with God.

So you've got these people who are in good grace with God because they've got Jesus and these people because they are Jews. We are breaking it down!

For this word works: "an act, deed, thing done," the idea of working is emphasized in opposition to that which is less than work. Let me say this to you folks. I am not here advocating anything against anybody. All I am saying is that everybody has to come to Him through the same Messiah. That's all that I am saying.

It doesn't matter who you are. I don't care what color you are. I don't care what land you live in. I don't care what your heritage is. I don't care who your mama is. The only way you come to my Elohim is through the Messiah He sent. It doesn't matter who you are.

You can say:

"Bailey is against this people."

I am against anybody that is not with Messiah. That's it. I don't care who they are, so don't get it twisted. There is only one group of people who are out there who think that they are "in" because of their ancestry. There are no other people out there. There is only one, and that is straight-up deception. How can I be a minister of the Almighty without calling it out for what it is, even though you may have a love affair with a view that is not even biblical?

Father is trying to get the Jewish people's attention. But as long as they think that they are all right rejecting this Messiah, they are going to end up in the same place every Gentile who rejects Messiah is going. And if you *really love* the Jewish people, you will tell them that. If you love anybody, you will tell them that.

So the use of Works: "work, one hundred and fifty-two times; deed twenty-two times, doing one time and labour one time." The word boast is another one:

"Lest any man should boast."

The word here is *kauchaomai* meaning: "to glory (whether with reason or without), to glory on account of a thing, to glory in a thing."

There are people who glory in being Jewish. I never understood this. I am having a conversation like:

"Hi my name is Arthur."

Or:

"Hi my name is ... and I'm Jewish."

And I could say:

"And your reason – why did you feel like you needed to tell me that? Why don't you just wear a kippah like everybody else so that I know that you are Jewish?"

I mean, I don't say:

"Hello, my name is Arthur and I'm Irish."

Most of the people you know will never even tell you where they are from. So why is it that certain people on the planet want you to know? It is because there is arrogance. There is pride.

"I'm the chosen. You're not."

I know what's going on. You might not. If I'm going to grab the tzitzit of a Jew, it is going to have a blue thread in it and they are going to be following Messiah. I'm not following any Jew who is not following Messiah because they won't end up where I want to go. So there are two requirements right there. They must be following Messiah and their tzitzits must have a blue thread in it.

We were in a store the other day. There were a couple of guys in there who had tzitzits almost down to their ankles. There were all white. There is a large population in the city of Charlotte and they wear all white tzitzits. It is like:

> "Wow, where is that at in the Bible? Why are you wearing tzitzits without blue threads?"

That is because if you are going to have tzitzits, shouldn't it have a blue thread in it? This lets you know that there are people who are supposed to be people of the book who don't follow the book. They are following some Rabbi, which Yeshua said:

> "Don't follow. Don't call anybody your teacher or your master."

But that doesn't stop Messianics from doing it. They do it gladly.

> "Well, my Rabbi..."

People who say that say it with a sense of arrogance. They are just prideful.

> "What are you proud of? What are you boasting about?"

To glory: that word glory means "boast, rejoice." Boasting is a form of rejoicing. There are times when you may be rejoicing. The Bible says to rejoice in YeHoVaH.

> "Well I can't rejoice. That's boasting. It might affect my salvation."

No it won't; not if you are doing it in the right context.

The doctrine or theology of grace did not come from Messiah, ladies and gentlemen; or Paul, but from Luther – Martin Luther and Westerners' theological interpretation of Luther, Paul and Messiah.

I'm going to show you that before Martin Luther came onto the scene, the Catholic Church believed in a salvation by grace and works! I'm going to show this to you.

Grace is a gift, but if I don't have to do anything, then this gift is extended to every person alive. Therefore every person on the planet will be saved by not having to do anything. We all know that is not true.

"We're saved by grace!"

Well, if I'm saved by grace and not of works, then every person on the planet is saved by grace because God told the world that He gave His only begotten Son. So all you have to do is to believe.

"Well, I believe!"

Oh ladies and gentlemen, when we get through breaking this down, folks are going to say:

"Well, I don't know. Am I saved?"

You see, this is why we don't have altar calls, ladies and gentlemen. We are disciples. That is what Yeshua said:

"Make disciples of the nations."

The church got it twisted. Now they want to have crusades and altar calls and "come to Jesus" meetings. But if people actually drink the Kool-Aid that they want to get other people to drink, they wouldn't be evangelizing. They wouldn't be all over the television and talking about taking the gospel. Why do you need to take the gospel anywhere?

You notice that you don't see Rabbis; Jewish Rabbis who don't believe in Yeshua, on TV. Do you notice that? The only time you see a synagogue service is during a High Holy Day and they may have put it onto YouTube. You don't see Rabbinics evangelizing. Only Christians do that.

Why are you evangelizing if you really believe that grace is a free gift? Because even as a free gift you have to do something just to receive it, just to accept it. How does the Almighty know that you have received it?

Some people will go to the Lake of Fire even though salvation is a free gift. How is that possible? I'm going to tell you something. There are these people who have had these revelations who say:

> "Nobody is going to the Lake of Fire."
>
> "Nobody is going to hell."
>
> "Everybody is saved."
>
> "Who would serve a God who would even think about doing something like that?"

Are you hearing me? Ladies and gentlemen, we've got so much work to do!

I'm going to be doing a message this Sabbath called: *It's Not Finished.* You see, we have to burst these bubbles. We've got to address it and make people see that from what you are interpreting from what was said, you have come away with the wrong interpretation.

So what is the right one? I can tell you that what you believe is wrong all day long, but I have to also show you what is right and then you can be the judge.

The whole point of courtrooms and lawyers is to really cause – if I can cause just a little doubt, then I now have people scratching their head. They are thinking:

> "You know, I'm not sure. I'm not sure. What I thought was an open and shut case isn't so open and shut any more."

It is supposed to be that way. You have jurors who are rushing to judgment and they are putting people on death row who are innocent; and letting people who are guilty go free. It is a shame when someone has been on death row for twenty or thirty years, only to find out that certain evidence was overlooked. Now this person has spent the majority of their life behind bars and they never should have been there in the first place.

Then you see all of these people walking free. Many of them should be locked up. People are quick to rush to judgment. Many people make a judgment from the news or from public opinion. Folks are arguing in internet chat rooms. They don't even have all of the evidence. They are putting out a dissertation on why they believe this person is guilty or why they believe this person is innocent.

Do you follow what I am saying? We do the same thing with the word. I've been guilty of it. I've made arguments based on perspectives that have been spoon-fed to me by my denomination only to later figure out that what I was fed was foam. It wasn't even real food.

This is where the bulk of the argument of:

> Eph 2:8 – "For by **grace** are ye **saved** through **faith**; and that not of yourselves: *it is* the **gift** of God: ⁹Not of **works**, lest any man should **boast**."

So it has gone from grace: you are saved through faith, to grace alone. Some people even go as far as faith alone. That's what Martin Luther did. Martin Luther went to faith alone. You're going to see this because that is when he addressed some issues. It literally changed the course of history.

If Martin Luther hadn't done what he did, everybody would be Catholic. Martin Luther protested against the Catholic Church. That is how the Protestant Reformation started. Now people are no longer Catholics. They are Protestants and they are denominational in their Protestant way of thinking.

One thing that Martin Luther did was that he saved people from going down the road of Catholicism. But when you begin to look at the issue that Martin Luther addressed, it was this whole issue of grace and faith and how it works together. I believe that he knew the definition of *saving grace.* I really believe he knew that.

Martin Luther did the Reformation and it was based on the just shall live by what? Faith. The just shall live by faith and not grace. It is "just." He is supposedly talking about people who have already been saved; so why do I now have to live a certain way if I am saved?

We are going to get into it ladies and gentlemen and break it down hopefully in a way where it is a simple thing of asking questions and sharing answers.

Chapter Two

This will address statements that people have made:

"We've fallen from grace."

Or:

"We're going under the law."

We are trying to explain and to communicate to folks. Inevitably the question comes up:

"What about grace?"

Recently we decided to specifically deal with that subject. We started this out from *Ephesians* chapter 2. This is the verse. Paul wrote *Ephesians* 2, but how many of you know that Paul wrote a whole lot more than *Ephesians* 2?

In *Ephesians* 2 we looked at:

> Eph 2:8-9 – "For by **grace** are ye **saved** through **faith**; and that not of yourselves: *it is* the **gift** of God: [9]Not of **works**, lest any man should **boast**."

We broke this down. We ended up on the word "boast" in verse 9. Recently we went through every one of these bold and underlined words in "What about Grace?" We didn't name it part 1, but this is part 2.

We mentioned also – and this is where we'll pick it up, on the doctrine or theology of grace. It did not come from Messiah. It did not come from Paul, but through Luther. It didn't come from Luther. It came through Luther and Westerners' theological interpretation of Luther, Paul and Messiah.

One of the things that you are going to see if you deal with denominational ministries or ministers or individuals in mainline, Presbyterian, Reformed, Lutheran or Methodist [circles] is this. You will find that these mainline denominations and even Baptists – mainline denominations have a tendency to go back to Luther.

They quote. What you hear them say is: "the Church Fathers." They always want to talk about the Church Fathers. What is interesting is that none of the Church Fathers are found in this book – none of them. They may be the Fathers of that church, but they are so far away from this book. They'll mention names you've never heard of.

What they have done is that they have gone out of the Bible. They have gone out of the Bible. Once they go out of the Bible, you've already lost the argument because it is not a biblical argument. It is a theological argument. We have to understand how to battle from a theological perspective.

Believe it or not, this is where logic comes in – not wisdom, logic. Now you have to get logical on folks. They are coming at you from a logical perspective; not from a spiritual or a biblical one, but from a logical one. Do you understand?

You cannot argue a spiritual argument with a logical person. You are talking here and you are going to continually miss each other. So now you have to identify what "logic bag" they are coming out of.

When it comes to the logic bag, that is where denominationalism comes in. Each denomination has a founder. The Catholics have a founder. The Lutherans have a founder. The Methodists have a founder. The Baptists, the Pentecostals – they all have a founder. From that founder down, there is still some adherence to the Church Fathers who supposedly founded them.

But by the time you get down to where we are today where the followers of that denomination and where the

Church Father was that established that denomination, there has been a lot of tweaking of the message.

You go into some places and they don't even know what denomination they are. That is because they are now full gospel or they are Charismatic or they are non-denominational. But even the non-denominations have an access point to a Church Father. So when people ask you what denomination that you are in, they are trying to identify your root into what you believe.

Once you associate yourself with a denomination, anyone who has denomination theological training already knows what you believe before you are even given an opportunity to explain what you believe. They say that if you are sitting in this denomination, then you are going to believe like this denomination believes, and it is a logical argument. You have to use logic in dealing with some of this.

The issue of grace: as I shared recently, when people start telling you and talking to you about grace, you have to ask them what they mean. You see, one of the things that I do is that I try to listen. I listen. I listen and listen because if I listen to you, you are going to tell me who you are. How am I going to know who you are if I am doing all of the talking?

People like talking. They want to tell you everything to help you understand them. The only way you are going to understand them is by listening. But guess what? You're trying to tell them everything they need to know to understand you. As soon as they catch their breath, you take over. When you catch your breath, they take over. You could have an hour or two hours of conversation and "nobody heard anybody." Do you understand what I am saying?

You have to be good listeners and you have to be good discerners. You don't want to spend an hour listening to somebody saying nothing. You have to discern. The gift of discernment, the Spirit of discernment is critical. Yeshua operated in discernment and the word of knowledge almost more than he operated in healing. He knew what a person was thinking. He knew where a person was coming from.

He cut the conversation into a third and went down the road that he knew the conversation needed to go in. The person got their answer and they went on their way. They may not have liked what they heard. So you need discernment.

When a person begins to talk about grace, then your first question should be:

"What do you mean?"

We looked at it. There are a lot of "graces" in the Bible. You can't have a conversation about grace until grace has been defined. You don't define it. Let them. What you are going to find is that they can't define it. If you are talking to somebody about a topic or a subject they can't define, how long do you think you are going to be in that conversation?

You'll be in there all day. They're just going around in circles talking about something that they can't even define. You think you understand it, so you're having a conversation thinking that you understand what they are talking about. But they don't have a clue what they are talking about. How are you going to have a clue?

Yeshua talked to the people in parables. Hearing, they didn't hear. Do you know why they didn't hear? It was because they already had their minds made up as to believing what they believe. People already have their minds made up to what they believe. When you come to them from a scriptural standpoint and you make a valid argument, do you know that the default is?

"Well, that's not what I believe."

"Okay, we could have got to that point an hour ago."

Why are we having an hour's worth of conversation only to find out that that is not what they believe? Why? It is because you have been trying to convince them of what you believe.

The first thing that you have to do is that you have to get on the same page. It is the same thing with husbands and wives. Once you get on the same page – the only way you get on the same page is that you have to have some candid discussion with some questions.

People say that Father (in the Bible) asked a lot of questions that He already knew the answer to. Now we know that He already knew the answer to it, so why is He asking the question? To see if you know the answer. That was the method that He used.

"Where are you Adam?"

As He is communicating to us, He is really trying to get us to see what is in us. What He wants to do is to help us to see what we are dealing with and what is in the person that we are trying to communicate with. It is not about trying to win an argument as much as it is about trying to get an understanding and to help people to get an understanding. You can get wisdom and you can get knowledge. With knowledge, you can get it a dime a dozen.

Get wisdom, get knowledge. But with all of your getting, what do you need? You need an understanding. My job is that if I can help a person to understand, then I am done. Now they have a dilemma. They have to figure out okay, now that they have the answer to the question – most times when people get the answer to the question, they don't like the answer. The reason why they don't like the answer is because the answer now requires a change.

Folks don't like change. They say they do.

> "Oh, tell me the truth brother. I want the truth and nothing but the truth."

Can you handle the truth?

> "Yeah, I can handle the truth!"

You give them the truth and it's like a sour face.

> "Wait a minute. I thought you said you could handle it!"

Grace – we know is a gift. If I don't have to do anything, then we know that this gift is extended to every person alive. Therefore every person on the planet will be saved by not having to do anything, and we all know that is not true. This is the argument.

> "Listen brother, you don't have to do anything. Grace is a free gift."

You can't earn it. You don't deserve it. Grace is extended to everyone because nobody can earn it and nobody deserves it, right? So how do you get it? It's a gift, right? So if it's a gift, then everybody has it. Do you see the logic in that? Now the person who wants to argue grace says:

> "No, wait a minute. That ain't right."

> "Well, that's what you are saying, isn't it?"

If it's a free gift and you don't have to do anything, the gift has been extended. Yeshua has died for the world. The gift of God has been given to the entire world. God so loved the world that He gave His only begotten Son. But get this, that *whosoever*, you see. So there is something that has to be done.

Some people will go to the Lake of Fire even though salvation is a free gift. How does that happen? This free gift is not of works and therefore I can't earn it nor do I deserve it. But how do I get it applied to me if I don't have to do anything?

See, these are the kinds of questions. If you notice, what I am doing is that I am putting question marks behind many of these because this is a logical argument. It is not a biblical argument, although it is scriptural. It is a logical argument.

Let me see if I've got this right:
1.) I don't have to accept the gift.
2.) I don't have to reject the gift.

Because it is a free gift, I don't have to do anything.

"Well now..."

Either you have to do something, or you don't!
So:
3.) I don't have to go to church.

Preachers won't like that!
4.) I don't have to obey anybody.

Now here is the other side of this illogical argument. If I don't have to do anything to get it, why do I have to do anything now that I've got it? I don't have to do anything. I don't have to go to church. I don't have to pay my tithes. I don't have to serve. All I have to do is to wait on Jesus.

I don't have to obey anyone. I mean, this is not even logical to an illogical person. I don't have to serve anybody. I don't have to do anything, nothing, nada. Why? Because I'm saved. Now if I do anything to be saved, then the free gift is nullified because I had to do something to get it.

You see, **the Bible doesn't preach that we are "saved by grace."** Folks like to shorten verses. **We're saved by grace through faith, not of works.** What is the definition of "works" and what is the Western concept of work? Now you are dealing with the issue of works. Folks want to associate:

"You're going to church on the Sabbath day brother. That's work. You're trying to earn your salvation."

"Oh, you want to keep the commandments, brother that is works. You're trying to earn your way to heaven."

"You've 'fallen from grace' if you have to do anything. Now you're getting into legalism."

It's like:

"Wow. Do you know what a covenant is?"

A covenant is a legal, binding agreement. You can't have a covenant without legality. You can't have legality without some kind of legalism. So yeah, I am a biblical legalist! We shouldn't be running from "legalism" if you understand covenant. Anybody who enters into a covenant – if any one of you of a Western mindset enters into a covenant, it is like a contractual agreement. Two sides agree. You receive a service or you receive some kind of product. You agree to pay for it.

If it is a service, you are going to pay for it as long as it is provided in good faith. When you buy something that is new, you get a warranty on it. If the warranty fails, guess what? You expect them to honor their agreement.

You get married and you have a covenant. You have a marriage license. You get a license, a driver's license. Before you get a license they say that you are going to have to pass this test. If you don't pass the test, you don't get the license.

And who does the license belong to? Your marriage license doesn't belong to you, it belongs to the state! Your driver's license doesn't belong to you, it belongs to the state. If you get a bar, if you are a mechanic, if you are a lawyer, whatever it is that requires you to get a license, you have to make sure that your license year after year after year is in good standing. Why?

That is because you don't own the license. The state owns it or the issuing organization owns it. They can revoke it. They can terminate it. They can disbar you. They can kick you out of the club.

So this word "work," let's look at it. When people say we are "saved by grace not of works," are they quoting the Bible or are they injecting their understanding of what the Bible teaches? That is what you have to get down to, because you need to know. When you make this statement, what do you mean? Now get this, ladies and gentlemen, you and I know that this verse is in the Bible.

> "Well, we're saved by grace brother through faith."
>
> "Are we? Are you banking on that?"
>
> "Yup!"
>
> "Well, where is that at in the Bible?"

The first thing that you have to do is to get people into the book. Don't have biblical conversations without the Bible. If you do, then you are now just a talking head. You are misquoting scriptures. You are throwing things out there. You are cutting and pasting. The first thing to do if you are going to talk about the word is to put the word in the midst of you.

> "Okay, let's crack the book."

If you are going to stand on this verse, then where is it at? At least show me where it's at. How are you going to have a conversation with a person about the Bible and the Bible is not even open? Then they say something really dumb like:

> "Well, I know that it's in the Bible. Do you know that verse where it says..."

Why would you answer that question and give them fodder or give them ammunition against yourself?

> "Well, you brought it up brother. You should at least know where it is at."

If you can't show me where it's at, why am I even talking to you? You have already determined that you are dealing with an ignorant person. Now I'm not trying to be mean, but if you ignore the fact that you are dealing with someone who is not knowledgeable about the conversation that they want to talk to you about, then the first thing that you need to do is to bring them up to snuff if they are willing to learn.

If they are not willing to learn, you've already identified that you are not only dealing with an ignorant person, but you are dealing with a person who has chosen to remain ignorant.

Shake the dust! Seriously, or you will be spending your time going around and talking in circles talking to someone who isn't even interested in what you have to say. They have already demonstrated that they are unwilling to learn. They want to talk about stuff that they don't even know what they are talking about. Why would you engage in that? Do you see the logic? They want to bring up a scripture and tell you:

> "Well, I know that scripture. Do you know where that scripture is? Do you know where that scripture is?"

> "Don't you? I mean, it's your argument."

You know there is nothing wrong with making a person talk. You are not trying to make them look stupid. They are doing that all by themselves. You are just helping them to see how stupid and ignorant they are looking.

Now you enter into stupidity and ignorance when you enter into a conversation with someone not even recognizing that you are dealing with someone who doesn't even know what they are talking about.

> "Well, I don't know the Bible."

> "Okay, well, when you learn, or would you like me to teach you? Would you like for me to help you learn?"

> "Well, uh hah. Praise the Lord."

Okay. I've picked your cards. I know who you are now and yet you will let these people hold you captive for hours and hours only to go over into default.

> "Well, that's not what I believe."

> "Well you know that in all of the conversations that we have had, do you even know what you believe? What do you believe?"

You see, that is something that you want to get to in the beginning. What do you believe? If I know what you believe, then that is a good place to start. We must ask when they throw that verse at us:

> "What do you mean? Please explain."

This is where the patience of the saints comes in! Are you hearing me? Look at that in a different light – the patience of the saints. It is not just being worn down. It is really dealing with people who are going to talk for hours, who really don't even know what they are talking about. But you are going to let them talk and let them talk. Eventually they are going to realize that they don't even know what they are talking about. Some will even go as far as to say – if you let people talk long enough, somebody will eventually say:

> "Well, I know I'm rambling now."
>
> "No, you've been rambling for the last half hour."

So it is:

> "What do you mean? Please explain."

"Work" has been defined by practitioners of the Christian faith in summary, as anything done that appears as one trying to earn God's favor or salvation.

If you go door-to-door like Jehovah's Witnesses, you are working. You are trying to earn your way into heaven. It's like, really? I'm not trying to justify what Jehovah's Witnesses do, but if you are going door-to-door to share your faith and you have the faith that was once delivered to the saints, then why not?

Now if you are bringing some other stuff like Watchtowers or Church Fathers material, then that is something to beware of. They say you are working if you are keeping the Law or any aspects of the Law like the Sabbaths or Feasts. Now you are working. You've "fallen from grace" because you don't have to do that stuff.

> "If I don't have to keep the Sabbath, why are you going to church on Sunday? Why? And why do you feel guilty when you don't go?"

It is not because the Bible has made you feel guilty. It is because the church has made you feel guilty.

> "Well, if I don't go to church brother, my week is just off."

Really? So now you are a trained parrot. You have to do this on Sunday or the rest of your week is just off. If you have the word in you and you are being led by the Spirit, how is not going to church on Sunday going to make your week off? That is a lot of faith in Sunday if it is going to affect your whole week!

Worshipping on Saturday – if you are worshipping on the Saturday Sabbath:

> "Oh brother, that's work!"
>
> "Okay, well, what do you call it when you worship on Sunday?"

If my worshipping on Saturday is "work," what is worshipping on Sunday called? Let's compare apples to apples. Let's drill down here a little bit. What about not eating things unclean like pork, shellfish or catfish?

> "Oh brother, you can eat anything!"
>
> "Oh yeah?"

So you can eat garbage now. You just put all kinds of junk into your body. Here's a little strychnine. There's some rat poison. Just pray over it! Do you know what I am saying? Yeah, put a little ketchup on it. [*Do not do this!*]

If you are going to associate things in the Bible with work, then explain to me what it means to "work out your own salvation?" See, obviously you haven't read that verse that Paul wrote, because he wrote it in *Philippians*.

> Phil 2:12 – "Wherefore, my beloved, as ye have always **obeyed**, not as in my presence only, but now much more in my absence, **work out** your own salvation with fear and trembling."

What are they obeying? Why do they have to obey anything? Now, don't just work out your own salvation, work out your own salvation with fear and trembling! Now wait a minute Paul, that's some heavy stuff right there. What happened to "we're saved by grace?"

> "Yeah, I did say that, but did you read the rest of it?"

What were they obeying? Paul doesn't explain it here, but he does explain it in his writings. For example, the apostles wrote considerably about obedience.

> Acts 5:32 – "And we are his witnesses of these things; and *so is* also the **Holy Ghost, whom God hath given to them that obey him.**"

Now who is giving it? The Almighty! To whom? Those who obey Him. Whom? God!

> "Wait a minute. What does God have to do with it? We believe in Jesus!"

You see, Yeshua came to reconcile! He is the mediator between God and man. That is who he is – the word.

> "Well, we just believe in the man."

No, the man was the word from the beginning. *Hebrews* 5:8. This always puzzled me, even when I was in the Baptist church. It's like how do I get my head around this one?

> Heb 5:8 – "Though he were a Son, yet learned he obedience by the things which he suffered;"

> Heb 5:9 – "And being made perfect, he **became the author of eternal salvation unto all them <u>that obey him</u>;**"

You see, I'm struggling as a Baptist. If we are saved – if we are "once saved always saved," then that says to me that no matter what I do, I'm good. I'm in. What is this obedience thing? What do I have to obey?

> "You all didn't tell me about obeying."

> "Well, you just have to obey the Pastor and the Deacon and the Mother."

Now wait a minute. You have people who now want to grab the scripture out of the command to Honor your Father and Mother. It was the first commandment with a promise that is mentioned by Paul in the New Testament; but separated from the Old Testament because this New Testament scripture came from the commandment.

> "So now you are saying that I don't have to keep the commandment. So I don't have to honor anybody. I don't have to honor my Mother and my Father."

> "Well, Paul said that in the New Testament."

Well, where did Paul get it from? He got it from the Torah!

> "So you are telling me that Paul is teaching from the Torah?"

You see, when you start asking questions, a lot of these dumb arguments go away. But if you are too busy trying to convince people of stuff when they already have their belief system, then the default is:

"Well, that's not what I believe."

You will always hit that.

"That's not what I believe."

The word he used here is *hupakouo,* meaning: to listen, to hearken. We get this hearken, to listen from the Hebrew word *Shema.* It's not just to listen, but to hearken; to obey.

The definition continues: "of one who on the knock at the door comes to listen who it is, (the duty of a porter); to hearken to a command; to obey, (to obey a command) to be obedient to, submit to."

So what are they obeying? What they've been commanded. Did Yeshua come to give a command that had not been commanded? Did he come to add to the Torah? Did Paul come to add to or to take away? No! They are obeying something. When you look at it, they are obeying something commanded.

Obeyed usage is to obey, to be obedient, to hearken. And then there is the *katergazomai,* meaning: to perform, accomplish, achieve; to work out.

When Paul talks about "working out your salvation," he is saying that you have to perform. There is something that is expected of you to achieve. Even Paul says that I have to fight the good fight. I have to run the race. There is a course that has been set before me. So he has to finish his course.

The idea of what he is saying is that your salvation is something that has been given to you that you now have to work out. But guess what? This grace that brings salvation has appeared to everybody.

Titus 2:11. This is the only biblical definition that comes straight from the Bible. So in *Titus* 2:11 it is very, very specific ladies and gentlemen. It says:

> Titus 2:11 – "For the grace of Elohim that brings salvation."

This is the saving grace. This is the saving grace.

> "...has appeared"

To who? All men. Shouldn't that be some? No, that's all. You see, grace is available. Saving grace is available to everybody. If it is available to everybody, how come some are going to be cast into the Lake of Fire? Obeying what?

You see, as you drill down in this argument, now you are asking questions. You are asking questions.

> "Okay, what does this mean? Okay, well obey what? Obey who?"

This is why people are more obedient to their Pastor than they are to the word. They are more concerned about being in good standing with the church. The church has made them believe that they are the representative of God on earth. Where did that come from? Catholicism! The Protestants are "half-baked" Catholics. You are going to see this here in just a minute.

The definition continues: "to perform, accomplish, achieve; to work out (i.e. to do that from which something results); of things: bring about, result in; to fashion i.e. render one fit for a thing."

He says here in *Titus* chapter 2:

> "...the grace of God that brings salvation has appeared to all men."

What does this grace do? This is not some free gift. This grace comes to teach you something! This is what Paul wrote. Paul wrote this! People want to take a verse from Paul and build a doctrine, instead of following Paul. If you want to follow Paul, follow Paul. Don't cut and paste Paul, follow Paul. By the time you are finished with Paul, Paul is going to say:

> "Hey, I keep the Law you all. Everything pertaining to the Law, I believe."

Paul would be looking at folks who are following him and say:

"What?"

Paul would have to figure out how to pull an "except you eat of my flesh and drink of my blood" number.

> "You all want to follow me, but you aren't following me!"

> "You want to take the fish and the loaves that I am handing out, but you don't want the word!"

You want to cut and paste. You want to take a little bit of this and a little bit of this and a little bit of that and build. It is amazing. The Baptists follow Paul just like the Pentecostals follow Paul, but they follow certain books from Paul. They follow certain teachings from Paul. They end up arguing using Paul against each other. It's like, how do you do that? I'm telling you. This is where you cannot abandon logic.

The usage of this work is: "to perform, the cause, to do a deed, to do deeds." Remember this word "deeds."

What is Paul talking about with obedience and why is Paul talking about obedience concerning our relation with God that is "by grace alone?"

People have misinterpreted Paul. If you follow what Paul is saying, that is a doctrine of the church. Paul didn't teach that. Yeshua didn't teach that. Luther didn't even teach that! Paul taught in *Romans* 1:

> Ro 1:4 – "And declared *to be* the Son of God with power, according to the spirit of

holiness, by the resurrection from the dead:"

Ro 1:5 – "By whom we have received <u>grace and apostleship</u>, for <u>obedience</u> to the <u>faith</u> among all nations, for his name:"

Ro 1:6 – "Among whom are ye also the called of Messiah Yeshua:"

Ro 15:18 – "For I will not dare to speak of any of those things which Messiah hath not wrought by me, to make the Gentiles obedient, **by word and <u>deed</u>**,"

Work! Gentiles have to work.

"Wait a minute brother, we're not saved by works."

Oh, yeah? That isn't what Paul said. Paul said we're saved by grace through faith, not of works. What is Paul addressing? Paul is addressing a people who have put their faith in their Judaism – their deeds, their good deeds, their good works. They didn't need Messiah, they had good works. Paul is saying:

"Listen, you need Messiah! Your works are not going to save you! You need Messiah!"

"No, we don't need Messiah, we've got works. We've got the Torah. We've got Moses. We've got Israel. We've got Abraham, Isaac and Jacob!"

"We're their seed. This Jesus? We don't know him. Who is he? Let his name be a curse!"

That's what they say. That's the word in the land.

> "Let his name be a curse or let his name be blotted out! 'Yeshu.' That's what he is. We don't believe in him and anybody who follows him is accursed."

Now you have Gentiles talking about how anybody who keeps those "Jewish" laws are cursed. They don't even know what they are talking about. Yeah, if you are following Judaism, you are cursed! That is because those who follow Judaism don't receive Messiah. They reject him! How can you have eternal life rejecting the Messiah who brought eternal life? You can't!

Paul taught that there are not only words that you have to obey. Like John said when he was baptizing in the Jordan; mikvahing in the Jordan and the Pharisees came to him. What did he say?

> "Bring works meat-worthy of repentence."

In other words, if you are receiving what I am saying, I'm going to see some change. Something is going to change. Even the people in the church who cry that "grace alone" stuff, if they have people among them who got saved and who don't change, they start looking at them with a raised eyebrow.

They are still looking for wolves in sheep's clothing. But how are you going to know a wolf? How are you going to know a wolf? It is one who says that they are a sheep, but they don't do what the shepherd says.

> "Oh, you have to do what the shepherd says now?"

As far as I'm concerned, you are all wolves! You're not following Messiah. What are you? The word here again is "deed." Paul says:

> Ro 15:18 – "...hath not wrought by me, to make the Gentiles obedient, **by word and..."**

Works. It is the same word – *ergon*. The Gentiles had to work their salvation out, just like the Jews. That's why there is no difference. Everybody had to work out their own salvation. It is not just in words. Don't just give me lip service. Yeshua says:

> "These people honor me with their lips, but their hearts are far from me."

How does he know their hearts are far from him? It is because what they do and what they say don't line up. You have people talking about how they are saved. How come you are living like the devil? You are talking about how you are saved, and you are living like the devil. Something is wrong with this picture.

How will you know them? By their fruit.

> "Why do they need to bring forth fruit? It's grace brother! You don't need fruit. You just believe."

> "Well, how do I know that you believe?"

How do I know that you are a believer? Because you tell me? Too many people have been hoodwinked.

> "Well, he says he is a believer Mama. He goes to church. He says he will come to our church when we get married."

> "Really daughter?"

> 2 Co 10:5 – "Casting down imaginations, and every high thing that exalteth itself against the knowledge of God, and bringing

> into captivity every thought to the **obedience** of Messiah;"

Now you have to work on your brain!

> "Well you know, praise the Lord. You know, I ain't there yet."
>
> "Uh huh. Well, how long are you going to be out there? You ain't there yet. Are you trying to get there?"
>
> "Well, you know, the Lord knows my heart."
>
> "Yes. That's why He wants to give you a new one – because the one you have stinks."

I mean, you know. Listen folks. There are people that you will talk to who really want to know the truth. They will ask you some hard questions, but they are not challenging you. Well, they are challenging you to give them truth, not to give them stuff, but to give them truth. They are not satisfied. When they hear the truth, they are going to go:

> "Oh."

That's because they have no argument for truth. They don't even know what it looks like. They don't even know what it sounds like. But when they hear it, it is like:

> "Oh."

You see, when you get an "Oh" moment, don't jump in. Just ease back. They are going to revel in that for a moment. Then they are going to come from a different angle. Then you give them another piece of truth. Then it is like (nods head Yes). Just leave it alone. Let it sit. If you give them too much, guess what? You are going to give them ammunition to go into a whole different direction and you just "pooped" on everything that you just did. Now you are in a whole different conversation.

That is how the enemy works amidst conversations, because we like to talk. And when you realize – you see, Yeshua didn't do a whole lot of that. He really didn't. When you know that you have given them something that they are going to have to get their head around, now it is time to hang up. Don't change the subject, it is time to go and talk to somebody else. Do you know what is going to happen? They will run back.

> "Do you know, when we were talking..."

Now they have some more questions. They have meditated on this and they tried to figure a way around it. That is what the human mind is going to do. The key is not to trap people, but to let people trap themselves. Once they have trapped themselves, now they are looking for somebody to help them get out of it. That is when they go to their preacher.

But if they are true about what they are looking for, they know when their preachers are blowing smoke. They know. They will try to hang out in that environment. Just because a person doesn't change because you have given them all of that truth, sometimes it takes weeks or months. Sometimes it takes a few years. The whole time they are in there wrestling, wrestling and wrestling. I have had people say:

> "You know, I've been listening to you for three years."

> "Really? Three years? It's the first time I've ever heard of you. It's the first time I've seen your name."

You have been listening for three years and you have never given an offering? Never had a prayer request? Never made a phone call? Never sent an email? But you have been listening for three years! I am not mad at you. But now you have surfaced. Why are you surfacing now after three years? What do you want? Oh yeah.

> 2 Co 10:6 – "And having in a readiness to revenge all disobedience, when your **obedience** is fulfilled."

Guess what? This word "obedience" is from the same "obey" which is this word *hupakoe,* meaning: obedience, compliance, submission. Obedience: rendered to anyone's counsel and obedience and observing (get this) the requirements of Christianity.

What are the "requirements of Christianity?" Now remember that we talked about how the people who wrote this stuff were Christians. They have put Christians in the Bible; all the way up to the New Testament gospel. Jesus was a Christian.

"Really?"

It is to obey, to be obedient. What did Yeshua mean when he said:

> Mt 5:16 - "Let your light so shine before men that they may see your good **works**, and glorify your Father which is in heaven"?

In other words he is saying:

> "If you are a follower of me, we are doing some work that people are going to see and they are going to say 'Man, that's good!'"

What are they going to do? They are going to glorify Him because of you. Why would they be glorifying Him because of you? It is because you are not doing works to glorify yourself. You are doing works to bring glory to Him. And if you do the works that He is calling you to do, guess who is going to get the glory from it? He is.

He used the same word in Paul's writing – not of works. Here is that word again, *ergon*. You are going to find this word throughout the Bible. Works, works, works, works, works, works, works.

> "Wait a minute brother. We don't have to do any work!"
>
> "Oh yeah? What Bible are you reading from? I know you are reading from the English translation, but have you bothered to..."

You see, the church defines works. The church has already defined works as "the Law." They didn't get this definition from the Bible. They got it from Christianity – the requirements of Christianity; whatever that is.

So now it is like:

> "What did Yeshua mean when he said 'Let your light shine so that men may see your good works?'"

What works is he talking about? Now they have to think about it.

> "Well, you know, when you feed the hungry..."
>
> "What do you mean feed the hungry? Why are you feeding the hungry? Why are you doing that? You don't have to do nothing."
>
> "Well now brother, it doesn't mean nothing-nothing."

> "Well what nothing does it mean? Help me to understand 'nothing,' because obviously you have a different definition of nothing than the definition I have; just like you have a different definition of 'work' than the work I've got. And you have a different definition of 'grace' than the grace I've got."

Don't throw me a word expecting me to understand your definition. I'm going to throw the word back at you to help me understand your definition. Now I know who I am dealing with. I know what grace I'm dealing with. I know what works I am dealing with. I know exactly what I am dealing with. From there I know how to go.

But I first have to identify who I am dealing with. Don't make the assumption just because you are using the same word, that you are using the same definitions applicable to those same words, because you are not.

The word here is business.

> "Let men see your good works."

The *work* here means: business, employment, that which any one is occupied; that which one undertakes to do, enterprise; undertaking; any product whatever, any thing accomplished by hand, art, industry, or mind; an act, deed.

There is that word deed again — in works and deeds. It also means: things done; the idea of working is emphasized in opposition to that which is less than work. So you are doing something.

There is so much that people read into the word instead of searching the word to understand what it is saying. It is not about what we want it to say or think it is saying, but what it is saying.

This is what we talked about in the Discipleship course – the difference between *eisegesis* and *exegesis*. Exegesis is to read the Bible and pull out of it, what is there. Eisegesis is when you take your denominational mindset and you read the Bible denominationally.

Whether you admit it or not, you do it. We all do it. You identify with certain passages of scripture. People even make the statement:

> "You know, that's my favorite verse right there."

> "You have a favorite verse? Really?"

So what does that mean? People will tell you something. A favorite verse is a default verse.

> "That is the verse that I go to whenever I'm in trouble or whenever I need comfort or whenever..."

It's like, Okay, that's wonderful. You have a favorite verse. If you have a favorite, then you might have some least favorites. I'm just saying. There are some you don't like because there are some you like. Guess what we do with the things that we don't like? We stay away from them. Oh yeah.

> "Well, that's not what that literally means."

> "Have you searched what that literally means? Then how can you say what it literally means? You mean what you understand it literally means based on what somebody told you it literally means."

I never really understood why preachers had to emphasize "literally."

> "Well, that's not what that verse *literally* says."

You know, that is a twenty-five cent word that to a person with a twenty cent mentality is a big word.

> "Well, that's not what that *literally* means."
>
> "Well, I'm ignorant. I don't know what it *literally* means. You explain it to me Pastor."

Hallelujah. Before I get into the rest of this, I want us to look at how Martin Luther and some of the others – but mainly Martin Luther. What did Martin Luther actually teach? What did he actually teach? The bottom line is that people want to attribute to Luther, things that Luther wouldn't take credit for if he was alive. You see, Luther understood.

Here is the other thing that you have to understand. The Catholics (which Luther was), believed very strongly in grace plus faith – grace plus faith, not grace alone. Luther didn't teach grace alone. That came from individuals' interpretation of what they wanted to make Luther say; based on what Luther said. But that is not what Luther taught. Luther didn't teach a grace-only doctrine.

Luther's favorite scripture in the Bible is found in *Romans* chapter one. As a matter of fact, I will leave you with this. It is something to chew on. *Romans* chapter one. This is the verse, this is the passage that Luther said. Martin Luther in his own writing, said that this changed his life forever.

> Ro 1:16 – "For I am not ashamed of the good news of the Messiah or the gospel of Yeshua Messiah, for it is the power of YeHoVaH [God] unto salvation to every one that believeth; to the Jew first, and also to the Greek; for therein is the righteousness

of YeHoVaH revealed, from faith to faith as it is written."

Paul here is writing "as it is written." It is written in the prophets. The just shall live by what? Faith. Luther's gospel became a faith alone gospel. Faith alone, not grace alone. He taught grace through faith, but he was interpreted as faith alone.

This is where people took Luther and then some said well, yes, faith. But he also taught grace. So faith alone, grace alone. Now there is a separation. You have the faith people and you have the grace people. The grace people aren't faith people. They are simply grace. The faith people aren't grace people. They're faith people.

You're going to see as we lay this out, that there are people who are walking by faith and they have their favorite verses. And there are people who are walking in grace and they have their favorite verses. If you listen to them, they will share with you all of their verses about grace. Then this group will show you all of their verses about faith. Rarely do they interact. They do, but rarely. We are going to look at that.

Chapter Three

Shalom! Today we're going to be picking up where we left off as we're dealing with the subject of grace.

"What About Grace?"

That is typically the refrain that people default to once you have cornered them and begin to share with them what the word actually teaches and they see it for themselves.

The foundational scripture that we have been looking at is *Ephesians* chapter 2, verse 8:

> Eph 2:8-9 – "For by **grace** are ye **saved** through **faith**; and that not of yourselves: *it is* the **gift** of God: ⁹Not **works**, lest any man should **boast**."

We have literally broken this down. We have looked at each of the key words in this particular passage: grace, saved, faith, gift, works and boast. We have given the actual definition of these words so that we don't assume or read into it, our own English definition or understanding.

What you will find is that people have actually taken this and they have made statements like:

> "You know, it's grace alone. We're saved by grace. It's grace only. Grace alone."

Some have taken it and said:

> "It's faith – faith alone."

Some people come along and say that:

> "Salvation is a gift."

What they have done is they have taken this particular passage, this particular verse and dissected these verses to make them align with a particular belief system that often times is not what Paul is writing nor what he is saying.

We're looking at this so that you will at least be able to understand what is being said here. When people take it and use it the wrong way, you can help them to see it the right way and virtually bring correction. It's not that you are trying to correct someone.

What you are doing is that you are bringing correction in a manner that hopefully will be such that adjustments will be made in the thinking of people. That way they will be able to apply the truth, versus the confusion that is surrounding these particular verses and passage – *Ephesians* 2:8 and 2:9.

We left off with the thought that concerns theology. The theology of grace did not come from Messiah. It did not come from Paul. Theology is the study of God. Man has established theology. Each man that establishes theological points of view – the founders of that theological point of view literally became the founders of a particular denomination or belief system.

That denominational belief system evolves into an organization that believes like that. When people begin to preach and teach, they establish followers. These followers are their disciples. This is what has happened throughout history. Individuals began to teach a particular doctrine or a particular teaching. They develop followers who like what they are teaching. They also develop opposition – people who don't agree. Those people develop followers.

Now you have a people who believe one way and a people who believe another way. Because of this theology and because of this doctrine, there are clashes. Sometimes these clashes lead to war – Holy Wars. These are people who are trying to force a particular doctrine; force a particular belief onto a particular society.

When people fight, they develop what you call governments. These governments develop rules and laws based on this doctrine; based on this theology and based on this belief system that now becomes law for a society.

All of this plays into it because the foundation of a lot of what you will find in societal law (they say) comes from the Bible and yet there are so many differences in how it is interpreted. The doctrine or theology of grace did not come from Messiah or Paul, but from Luther and Westerners' theological interpretation of Luther, Paul and Messiah.

You are going to find ladies and gentlemen, that besides Paul, Luther is the most influential person on the planet as it relates to Christianity. You are going to see that things that Luther wrote way back when are still at play today. You are going to hear phrases and statements that Luther made, that are now in sermons.

Historically, three groups emerged outside of Judaism. They are the Catholics, the Protestants (Protestants evolved into what are called Lutherans). Lutherans are really Catholic Reformers. Luther was a Catholic all of his life. Luther was never a Lutheran. He was a Catholic and he stayed a Catholic. The third group of people is the Anabaptists. Anabaptists are an offshoot of Protestantism.

Catholics claim their authority from Peter as being the first Pope. Protestants are hybrids or "mutant" Catholics which claim their authority from Martin Luther. Then you have the Anabaptists who consider Anabaptism to be an offshoot of Protestantism. Others see it as a direct movement. The Amish, Hutterites and Mennonites are direct descendants of the movement. Then there is Schwarzenau Brethren, Bruderhof and the Apostolic Christian Church. These are later developments in Anabaptist groups.

Get this. The name "Anabaptist" means "one who baptizes again." You many not hear the term Anabaptist, but you are exposed to it. When you go from one denomination to another denomination, if you have been baptized in a former denomination, they say you must be what? Baptized again. Now you have people who come into the Hebrew Roots movement and who because of this philosophy that has been incorporated into them feel that:

> "Okay, I was baptized as a Baptist. I was baptized as a Catholic. I need to be baptized as a Messiahan. I need to be baptized as a Messianic. I was baptized in Jesus' name. I was baptized in the name of the Father, Son and Holy Ghost. Now I need to be baptized in the name of Yeshua."

That is the doctrine of the Anabaptists that has been incorporated into theology. The Anabaptists felt that if you were baptized as an infant, you were not of the age of accountability to where you made the decision to be baptized yourself. Now you see this thing emerging. You have many people within the church communities who reject infant baptism. They make statements like:

> "A person shouldn't be baptized until they are able to accept Yeshua or Jesus themselves."

They don't even realize that this thinking came from the Anabaptists way back yonder during the Reformation. That theology exists among people today in all walks of life and in all denominations. It is certainly adhered to in denominational congregations.

This name (Anabaptist) was given them by their persecutors in reference to the practice of rebaptizing converts who already had been baptized as infants. Anabaptists required that baptismal candidates be able to make their own confessions of faith, so they rejected infant baptism.

What you are going to find is that many people have a myriad or a mixture of various theological arguments that have been deposited into their spirit. When you sit under a teaching and you open yourself up to a teaching, things are being deposited in your spirit that affect your belief system and shape your doctrine.

When you begin to communicate, you begin to communicate what you believe. What you believe often times may not necessarily be sound, but it is what you believe. This is what happens with people when you begin to show them what the Bible teaches and their default is:

> "Well, that's not what I believe."

Once you are able to put that mirror in front of them concerning their belief system, what happens?

> "Well, what about grace? What about grace brother? Now you want to put works on me!"

The person who has had the greatest impact on faith and the modern church is Martin Luther. Although people don't preach Martin Luther, they come at you with the term:

> "Church Fathers."

Have you ever heard that one?

> "Church Fathers."

Whenever people use "Church Fathers," they are not talking about anybody in this book. They have already taken you out of the Bible. That is what they have done. When they have taken you out of the Bible and they want to preach the "Church Fathers" to you, what they are saying is that the way that these individuals interpreted this book is where we have put our mark in the sand. It is their interpretation of the book.

You would think that Church Fathers would be in the book. Why aren't they in the book? It is because the church is not in the book. The word "church" is you see, but that is an evolution. These individuals want you to think that Christians were all the way back at Pentecost in Jerusalem during the Feast of Shavuot or the Feast of Weeks.

> "Well, on the day of Pentecost, that's when the church was born!"
>
> "Yeah, really?"

That's what they say. That's what they argue and that's what people believe. They have been making this argument for several hundred years – at least for 1,700 years.

Luther taught that salvation and subsequently eternity in heaven is not earned by good deeds, but is received only as a free gift of God's grace through faith in Jesus Christ as redeemer from sin and subsequently eternity in hell. You could say that what Luther is saying is good. You can support this – that salvation and eternity in heaven is not earned. You can't earn it. We agree to that.

You can't work for it. It can only be received and there is the key right there. You have to receive it. Now, some can argue and have argued successfully that to receive it is an action. Any action violates the "freeness" of it. You see, I can give you something, but you can reject it or you can accept it. You have a will that is incorporated into the acceptance or rejection of this free gift. If a free gift is forced on someone, it is no longer a gift.

Salvation is not forced on anyone. Anybody can accept it. Anybody can reject it and thus it is an action on their part. Luther writes this. Ultimately he comes out against free will. He rejects the notion that free will is involved. God is doing all the work. God is now – I want you to think about this logically. God comes at you. He gives you His word. He gives you faith by grace and then He puts His

Spirit on you. Now by His Spirit you can receive this word of faith by grace.

It's the Almighty that's bringing the word. It's the Almighty that's overshadowing and overpowering you and giving you the ability to receive this word totally void of any action on your part. And if that be the case, why doesn't He do it with everybody? Do you follow me? If that is how He works, then everybody on the planet will be saved. Why? Because that is His desire. His desire is that all men be saved.

So if He is only doing it to certain people and not doing it to other people, then He is now a respecter of persons. The argument doesn't hold up when you address the argument from a logical point of view. Either He is going to do it to everybody or He is choosing who He is going to do it to. This is where the Calvinists come away with the whole idea of election – the doctrine of election.

The doctrine of election says that certain people are going to be saved. The elect are the ones that God chooses. There are some that are going to go to hell because they are not elect. Well, how do you decide who's the elect and who is not the elect? You are the elect if you are born into this denomination. You now have to be part of this denomination, because "the elect" are part of this group.

Anyone who is outside of this group is not the elect. This is where it gets really weird. There are some that are the elect who believe that they have to evangelize and tell people about the good news so that they can receive it. Then there is another elect; which is among the Presbyterians and among the Calvinists.

The Calvinistic model; the Wesleyan model says that:

> "Well, no, you don't have to tell people about this because God has already chosen who is going to be saved and who is not going to be saved."

That's predestination. But then when you begin to try to drill down into that, the question becomes:

> "So are you saying that man has absolutely no say in whether he is going to be saved or not – none?"

Believe it or not ladies and gentlemen, this is the very argument that Yeshua had to deal with, with the Pharisees and the Sadducees. When he was dealing with the Jewish people of his day, they would say:

> "Listen, we're Abraham's seed. We are Abraham's seed, so we are the elect of God and we don't have to do anything. We were born into this."

Whether you know it or not, when a person says to you without you inquiring:

> "I'm Jewish."

That is what they are saying.

> "Hi, my name is whatever and I'm Jewish."
>
> "Okay."

Now you may not know what is going on, but they are saying to you:

> "I'm the chosen one. I'm the chosen one. You better know this. I'm Jewish. I'm proud of it! Why? Because I am one of the chosen people. As a chosen one, I don't need that Jesus. I don't need that 'may his name be blotted out' guy. I'm Jewish."

Luther's theology challenged the authority and office of the Pope by teaching that the Bible is the only source of divinely revealed knowledge from God. He opposed **sacerdotalism.**

This word is an interesting word. By considering all baptized Christians to be a holy priesthood, what Catholicism did is that it ushered in a replacement theology. It didn't identify itself as replacement, but what it did was that it now hijacked a priesthood system from the Jewish people and applied it to the followers of Messiah.

The Pope is the "High Priest." Then you have the priesthood. These are the Cardinals and the Bishops, the Archbishops. Those individuals were like the Levites. You have the Pope and you've got the Priests and the Levites (if you would). These are the individuals that replaced Judaism for the sake of Catholicism. Therefore you now have this hierarchy going on.

This hierarchy of *sacerdotalism* is defined as a belief that propitiatory sacrifices for sin require the intervention of a Priest. Now the people had to come to a Priest to make their confessions. They no longer had to bring an animal sacrifice.

They no longer had to bring any kind of sacrifice for their doings. They just had to do penance. Penance in Catholicism got to a place where they were selling restitution or penance. They were selling these things to people who were able to now buy forgiveness (if you would). I mean, that is what it really boiled down to. That is the belief that a special, segregated order of men called the priesthood are the only ones who can commune directly with God or the gods.

The system of the papacy replaced the system of the Levitical priesthood. It established another priesthood that was Catholic and which claimed Pope Peter as the founder or as the head or as the first Pope.

Those who identify with these and all of Luther's wider teachings are called Lutherans **even though Luther insisted on *Christian* as the only acceptable name for**

individuals who professed Christ. That is what he insisted on. Today, Lutheranism constitutes a major branch of Protestantism and overall Christianity with some 80 million adherents.

The fact that followers of Luther called themselves "Lutherans" is clear evidence of a departure from Luther's beliefs and teachings. Luther did not set out to establish Lutheranism. Luther was a Catholic. Luther wanted the Catholic Church to reform. Instead of reforming the Catholic Church, he started what people have now theologically dubbed, a reformation. A reformation that is now called a Reformation – a Reformation that was established with Luther at the helm.

Luther became convinced that the church was corrupt in its ways and had lost sight of what he saw as several of the central truths of Christianity. The most important for Luther was the doctrine of justification. This is God's act of declaring a sinner righteous by faith. Now there it is – *by faith alone through God's grace.*

What you are going to see here ladies and gentlemen is that it *was* grace through faith. *It evolved into* faith alone through God's grace. Then it got to where Luther wrote faith alone. Luther came to understand justification as entirely the work of God.

This teaching by Luther was clearly expressed in his 1525 publication *On the Bondage of the Will*, which was written in response to *On Free Will* by Desiderius Erasmus (1524). Theologians will recognize these names because they have studied them.

Erasmus admired Luther and Luther admired Erasmus. Erasmus was a scholar. Luther was also a scholar, but Erasmus simply wanted to be scholarly. He did not want to be part of any movement. You are going to see that this created a problem for Luther.

Luther based his position on predestination on St. Paul's epistle to the *Ephesians* 2:8-10. We read chapter 2, verses 8 and 9. Of course he uses verse 10, so let's read verses 8-10.

> Eph 2:8-10 – "For by grace are you saved through faith; and that not of yourselves, *it is* the gift of YeHoVaH; not of works, lest any man should boast, for we are his workmanship, created in the Messiah unto good works, which Elohim has before ordained that we should walk in them."

So what you are going to see – remember that I gave the illustration. You will see that Americans have a tendency – not just Americans, but now the world has a tendency to begin to reduce letters and names to an acronym. You have a good example with the Young Men's Christian Association. That became the "YMCA." That became the "Y."

With texting and with ebonics, you will find that people are now using letters like "LMAO" or "LOL" or "OMG." This is the society that we live in. Now it is like people are too lazy to sound out words or they have too many words to say, so they just use the acronym. They expect that you know the language.

> "What do you mean you don't know the language? Oh, you must be old school!"

You see?

> "Old school."

It is like the Old Testament. You are outdated, old and have lost your use and value.

Desiderius Erasmus wrote that:

> "Free will does not exist according to Luther."

So now they are writing. There is a writing war that is going on between these two gentlemen. Both of them are impacting society as we know it way back then. The effects of what they wrote and did way back then in the 1500s is still with us today.

He wrote:

> "Free will does not exist according to Luther"

...in his letter *De Servo Arbitrio* to Erasmus that was translated into German by Justus Jonas (1526). In that letter, he stated that sin makes human beings completely incapable of bringing themselves to God.

This is how this translates into Calvinism. It is called the complete degradation of, or to be completely deprived. Man is completely deprived of any ability to do any right. Therefore he does not have the ability to come to God on his own or even to receive the grace of God. This is why it has to be given as a free gift; totally void of man's interaction. Man doesn't have to do anything, but to receive something is doing something.

They will even go to the point where you can't come to a place where you ask God to come into your life. They will say that that is the work of the Evangelical. The Evangelicals came up with a doctrine and a teaching to where now comes the fiery brimstone; Evangelical hell brimstone message where it scares a person into making a confession of faith.

Luther is saying that human beings are completely incapable of bringing themselves to God. They have absolutely no ability because of their complete depravity.

Erasmus described Luther as:

> "A mighty trumpet of gospel truth"

...while agreeing:

> "It is clear that many of the reforms for which Luther calls are urgently needed."

When Erasmus hesitated to support Luther however, the straightforward Luther became angered that Erasmus was avoiding the responsibility due to either cowardice or a lack of purpose. Do you see this writing war? They are going at each other. They both have access to the same audience. Whenever you have access to the same audience, it is like this:

> "You are either going to come onto my team – we're going to do this thing together or I am going to cut you up."

What does that do? Now the people are going to have to make a choice as to who they are going to follow. And there you go, it is a split.

To Philip Melanchthon in 1524, Erasmus wrote these words:

> "I know nothing of your church;"

These guys are trying to get him onto the same team. He says:

> "Listen, I know nothing of your church; at the very least it contains people who will, I fear, overturn the whole system and drive the princes into using force to restrain good men and bad alike. The gospel, the word of God, faith, Christ, and Holy Spirit – these words are always on their lips; look at their lives and they speak quite another language."

He is writing this in the 1500s. He is saying that these people are preaching this gospel with love, or they are saying things like the gospel, the word of God, faith, Christ, the Holy Spirit. But their lifestyle is totally contrary to the words that they are speaking. Now understand that Luther is watching the opulence of the Catholics and he is saying:

> "You know, you guys are all about money. You are using your position of power to rape the people, to pillage the people, to fleece the people. The people are totally ignorant of what it is that you are doing because you have put yourself as a people of authority – religious authority over the people. You have usurped the power and the authority over the people. Now the people have to see you as the representative of God in the earth."

That spirit is alive today in all denominations. Whether you like it or not, people try to force their ministers into that place.

> "How come you let people call you 'Arthur'?"
>
> "Well, that's what my Mama calls me. It's on my birth certificate."

You have people who say:

> "Well, I'm the Reverend..."
>
> "Okay, let me see your license."

Is "the Reverend" on your birth certificate? Is "Doctor" on your birth certificate? Is "Doctor" on your driver's license? If you want people to call you – when people introduce themselves as:

> "I'm Doctor So and So. I'm Reverend So and So. I'm Bishop So and So. I'm Pastor So and So."

It is like:

> "Okay. How do you introduce yourself like that, when the fact of the matter is that now you are saying that a title is part of your name?"
>
> "I'm Mister. Call me 'Mr. Bailey'. Don't call me 'Arthur'. Call me 'Mr.'"

Do you see? Anyway, he is saying that:

> "You people are saying one thing, but your lifestyle is saying something else."

Then in 1529 he writes an epistle. An epistle ladies and gentlemen, is a letter. Paul wrote epistles. So he writes *An epistle against those who falsely boast they are Evangelicals.* Now he is attacking Evangelicals. He says to Vulturius Neocomus (Gerardus Geldenhouwer) – here Erasmus complains of the doctrines and morals of the Reformers.

Luther was a Reformer, but these guys are like contemporaries. They are side by side. They know each other. They are watching each other. Erasmus is not trying to recruit Luther, but Luther is trying to recruit Erasmus because he sees the scholarly ability and the influence that Erasmus has over the people; and he is a writer. He is a scholar. He is a theologian. He is recognized as an authority and people listen to him.

So by building on that relationship, Luther empowers and makes himself that much more accepted and heard. People are saying:

"Well, if Erasmus is with him, wow. Okay. I'm with Erasmus. If Erasmus is with him, then he is endorsing him. So he must believe him. Since I follow Erasmus and Erasmus is following Luther, then I am going to follow Luther."

He says:

"You declaim bitterly..."

This is what he is writing against the Reformers whom he considers to be Evangelicals. He says:

"You declaim bitterly against the luxury of priests,"

You see, the priests were living luxurious lives. When you see all the pomp and revelry, I'm telling you right now. There are people in the Catholic Church that are living in million dollar mansions all over the United States. They just exposed some a year ago. Chicago, Philadelphia, Massachusetts, California – the new Pope had to come out against a lot of it. He is saying that:

"You people are living too high on the hog to be considered priests."

This was way back in the 1500s. It was even worse than that. Now it is kept a lot more secret, but one of the richest organizations on the planet is the Catholic Church. It is so much so that it has its own state, its own zip code, its own laws and its own bank.

"You declaim bitterly against the luxury of priests,"

Luther...

"the ambition of bishops,"

Luther...

> "...the tyranny of the Roman Pontiff and the babbling of the sophists; against our prayers, fasts and masses; and you are not content to retrench the abuses that may be in these things, but must needs abolish them entirely."

> "Look around on this 'Evangelical' generation and observe whether amongst them less indulgence is given to luxury, lust, or avarice than amongst those whom you so detest."

In other words, he is saying that the very people who are joining your fight are living just like the people who you are fighting against. Everybody wants to be on the ground floor of the movement. If I am on the ground floor of the movement, I get to sit on the right hand or I get to sit on the left. I've got a place of honor in the movement.

> "Show me any one person who by that gospel has been reclaimed from drunkenness to sobriety, from fury and passion to meekness, from avarice to liberality, from reviling to well-speaking, from wantonness to modesty."

> "I will show you a great many who have become worse though following it...The solemn prayers of the church are abolished, but now there are very many who never pray at all..."

You will find that when people came into the Hebrew Roots movement who used to be in Pentecostalism, many people in Pentecostalism prayed in tongues more. They fasted more. They may have felt that their relationship was stronger. But when they come into this, often times the move and work of the Spirit ceased in their lives.

What he is saying is that these people used to pray, but now that they are rebelling; they are protesting and they are coming under a new spirit. They are not praying the rosary. They are not praying at all. Now they are reevaluating everything that they believe. He says:

> "I have never entered their conventicles, but I have sometimes seen them returning from their sermons, the countenances of all of them displaying rage and wonderful ferocity, as though they were animated by the evil spirit…"

I'm thinking that I've come to a point where I can't make fun of them or talk about them. I feel sorry for them. When I see well-known preachers, I want to ask them sometimes:

> "Do you think that Yeshua preached like that? Do you think that he did all of that animation? All of that performance to get the people rattled?"

People like it. People love it. People in those denominations; in many of the Baptist churches and many of the Pentecostals and the Sanctified churches love when the ministers go into that "preach" mode, that hoot mode. They feel that now he is preaching. He wasn't preaching before, but now he's preaching.

Folks want to stand up and they want to get their look. They want to "Amen" and they want to rock and sway and do all of those kinds of things because now the preacher just started preaching. We've been talking all this time, but now he's got that preach on.

"Preach preacher!"

Then you see the women. Folks start getting that look on their face like:

"Ooooh this is GOOD!"

You see these faces. It's like:

"Really? Is that what the Spirit does? The Spirit just contorts your face like that?"

If you are honest, you will see that some of these people look like they have a demon. They look like their face is all contorted. That is a "holy" look to them. This is what Erasmus is saying. He is saying:

"Look at them — their countenance."

"...the countenances of all of them displaying rage..."

They are looking MEAN!

"...as though they were animated by the evil spirit..."

"Who ever beheld in their meetings any one of them shedding tears, smiting his breast, or grieving for his sins?...Confession to the priest is abolished, but very few now confess to God..."

"I don't need to confess to nobody! It's just God and me. That's the only one I need to ask forgiveness for."

Well, when you sin against men, you ask men for forgiveness.

> "Well, I don't need to ask no man for forgiveness because this is just between me and God."

Well, God says that if your brother sins against you, that you go to him.

> "Well, where is that at in the Bible?"

You see, you are not even reading the Bible any more.

> "Well, I don't believe that!"
>
> "What do you mean you don't believe that?"
>
> "Well, that's not what I believe."
>
> "Oh, so you don't believe what the Bible says?"

This is why we've come to a place ladies and gentlemen, in Bible society where people don't follow the steps of restoration. They don't go to their brother. They look to everybody for advice on how to address their brother.

> "What do you think I should do? My brother did this..."

The Bible says to go to him and him alone. Why are you talking to everybody else?

> "Well, I'm just trying to get some wisdom on how to go to him. I'm just trying to get some wisdom on how to go to him."
>
> "Why do you need to get wisdom? The wisdom is in the word. Why aren't you doing what the word says? That is where the wisdom is at. How do you expect the

Almighty to honor what you are doing if you are not doing what He says to do? You go another way."

"Well, he's not going to listen!"

"Well, take two more."

"Well, it don't take all of that. I'll just cut him off."

This is what he is addressing way back then. You see, what he is saying is that the Catholic Church may have some things off, but let's compare the people who have protested against the things that are off in the Catholic Church. Let's look at their lives and compare it to the lives of the people who are still there. You have people who are there. They are going to confession. You have people there who are smiting their breast. They are recognizing their sinful condition; which leads them to confession.

You have people who have protested against all of that. You are not confessing your sins. You are not smiting your breasts. You are not even acknowledging your sin because you are too mad at the people who are doing the things that they are doing. It is like everything that they are doing is wrong. This is what he says:

"Whoever beheld them. They are not confessing."

"Very few now confess to God. They have fled from Judaism that they may become Epicureans."

Now what is an Epicurean? **Epicureanism** is a system of philosophy based upon the teachings of the ancient Greek philosopher Epicurus, founded around 307 BCE. You can look that up. I just gave you that. Epicurus believed that what he called "pleasure" is the greatest good, but the way to attain such pleasure is to live modestly and to gain knowledge of the workings of the world and the limits of one's desires.

This is almost like the Catholics. Here you have people who supposedly have taken a vow of poverty, but they are living more opulent. It is like, how do you take a vow of poverty and live like a king?

Then you have these individuals who are saying that you have to live modestly; and that is good, but you can't tell people how to live. You can't. You can teach them what the Bible says. The Bible talks about modesty in dress. It talks about modest living. But to take that and for yourself to now define modesty, you can't.

> "Continuing his chastisement of Luther – and undoubtedly put off by the notion of there being 'no pure interpretation of scripture anywhere but in Wittenberg'"

Luther didn't intend for this to happen, but this is what happened. Luther is saying that these people; all of them are misinterpreting the Bible. The only person who has a proper interpretation of the Bible is himself. Erasmus says:

> "Listen man. You are saying that the notion of there being no pure interpretation of scripture anywhere but in Wittenberg..."

That is where Luther was. Erasmus touches upon another important point of the controversy. He says:

> "You stipulate that we should not ask for or accept anything but Holy scripture, but you do it in such a way as to require that we permit you to be its <u>sole interpreter, renouncing all others. Thus the victory will</u>

<u>be yours if we allow you to be not the steward, but the lord of Holy scripture."</u>

That is exactly what denominationalism does. It goes into a whole other realm. In his catechism (entitled *Explanation of the Apostles' Creed*) – how many of you have ever heard of the Apostles' Creed? It wasn't written by the Apostles. It was just given a name so that you would *believe* that it was from the Apostles. Not one apostle was involved in the writing of the Apostles Creed – not one.

Erasmus took a stand against Luther's teaching by asserting the unwritten *sacred tradition* as just as valid a source of revelation as the Bible. He did this by enumerating the deuterocanonical books in the canon of the Bible and by acknowledging seven sacraments.

Now the deuterocanonical books are other books. There are a lot of them. He called "blasphemers," anyone who questioned the perpetual virginity of Mary. This is Erasmus. However, he supported lay access to the Bible. In a letter to Nikolaus von Amsdorf, Luther objected to Erasmus' catechism and called Erasmus a "viper." Now they are turning on each other. He called him a "liar" and:

"the very mouth and organ of Satan."

This was because Erasmus didn't join forces with Luther. Luther at first wanted him to join forces with him. But because Erasmus took a stand and did not join forces with him and called him out on some of the things that were done, now he has to cut him up. He has to break him down. He has to make him look like a demon, a monster and a person opposed to God.

Erasmus was accused by the monks against the Reformation that he had prepared the way and was responsible for Martin Luther. Erasmus (they said) had laid the egg and Luther hatched it. But Erasmus wittily dismissed the charge, claiming that Luther had hatched a different bird entirely.

What Luther brought in he said – he admired what Luther brought in. But by the time that Luther finished, what Luther had brought forth did not look anything like anything that he had anything to do with.

Luther and the Law

Early in 1537, Johannes Agricola (1494-1566), serving at the time as pastor in Luther's birthplace Eisleben, preached a sermon in which he claimed that God's gospel not God's Moral Law (the Ten Commandments), revealed God's wrath to Christians.

Based on this sermon and others by Agricola, Luther suspected that Agricola was behind certain anonymous antinomian theses circulating in Wittenberg. (Antinomian is anti-law.)

These theses asserted that the Law is no longer to be taught to Christians, but belonged only to city hall. This is where Christianity is today – that the Law belongs to city hall. It teaches that the only laws that we are governed by are the laws of the court – the laws of the land, the laws of man. We are no longer under the Law of God. This was way back in the 1500s. These are the "Church Fathers."

In his theses and disputations against the antinomians, Luther reviews and reaffirms on the one hand what has been called "the second use of the Law." That is the Law as the Holy Spirit's tool to work sorrow over sin in man's heart, thus preparing him for Christ's fulfillment of the Law, offered in the gospel.

Luther states that everything that is used to work sorrow over sin is called "the Law," even if it is Christ's life, Christ's death for sin, or God's goodness experienced in creation. I am using these terminologies because that is the terminology he used. Luther didn't refer to Yeshua Messiah as Yeshua Messiah, but as Jesus Christ.

Simply refusing to preach the Ten Commandments among Christians – thereby as it were, removing the three letters l-a-w from the church – does not eliminate the accusing Law! He says:

> **"You can take the Law out of the church, but the Law is still there!"**

Claiming that:

> **"The Law in any form should not be preached to Christians anymore"**

...would be tantamount to asserting that Christians are no longer sinners in themselves and that the church consists only of essentially holy people. What is Luther saying? *Luther is saying that you can't remove the Law*! The Law has a place in the church! The followers of Luther, if they truly followed Luther, would be following Luther.

Do you know what else? Calvinists are people who follow John Calvin. John Calvin believed that the commandments of God are supposed to be a part of the believer's life. Luther believed it. Calvin believed it. But the followers of Luther and the followers of Calvin have evolved so far away from them that they reject what the founders believed.

In his own writings – I had Calvin commentaries. I don't have them anymore. When Calvin commented on *Matthew* chapter 5; when he talked about how Yeshua (Jesus) didn't come to do away with the Law, he did a long commentary on what Yeshua meant. He believed that the Law was a part of the believer's life and that if you remove the Law from the believer's life, you have just damaged the gospel message. This is what Luther taught.

On the other hand, Luther also points out that the Ten Commandments when considered not as God's condemning judgment but as an expression of his eternal will, that is of the natural Law, also positively teach how the Christian ought to live.

What Luther did in one sense is that he stood by the Law. But in another sense, he downgraded the Law. The reason why people do this is because when people start asking questions, either we keep the Law or we don't keep the Law. What Law do we keep? Well, we do keep the Ten Commandments. What Luther is advocating here is the Ten Commandments. That is what is considered as "the Law."

Calvin advocated the Ten Commandments. Lutherans read the Ten Commandments every evening service. They read two things; either the Apostles' Creed or the Nicean Creed. If you know anything about creeds, there are three main ones. These are the Apostles' Creed, the Nicean Creed and the Athanasian Creed. These are the three main creeds in Catholicism and Lutheranism. You can look these up: Athanasian Creed, Apostles' Creed and Nicean Creed.

One of these creeds, either the Nicean or the Apostles' Creed is read in every Lutheran evening vesper; evening service. I've never been to a Catholic evening service, but I believe that the Catholics recite the Ten Commandments. I know that the Lutherans do because I was once a minister in it and we did it in every evening service – all of the Lutherans in the Missouri Synod Lutheran church.

Here we are confessing that we are to remember the Sabbath day and to keep it holy, while at the same time teaching that the Sabbath is Sunday. So now you have the Christian Sabbath. All of this didn't come from Luther.

This has traditionally been called the "third use of the Law." *For Luther, Christ's life, when understood as an example, is nothing more than an illustration of the Ten Commandments*; which a Christian should follow in his or her <u>vocations</u> on a daily basis (that means that if you really believe that the Sabbath is valid, according to his own teachings and beliefs).

Luther and Anti-Semitism

Luther wrote about the Jews throughout his career, although only a few of his works dealt with them directly. Luther rarely encountered Jews during his life, but his attitudes reflected a theological and cultural tradition which saw Jews as a rejected people guilty of the murder of Christ. He lived within a local community that had expelled Jews some ninety years earlier.

He considered the Jews as blasphemers and liars because they rejected the divinity of Jesus; whereas Christians believed Jesus was the Messiah. Luther believed that all human beings who set themselves against God were equally guilty.

He had an anti-Semitic approach. As early as 1516, he wrote that many people:

> "...are proud with marvelous stupidity when they call the Jews 'dogs, evildoers' or whatever they like, while they too and equally, do not realize who or what they are in the sight of God."

You will find that Luther used a lot of vulgarity – I mean cuss words. Luther provoked his audience and spoke violently. You are going to see some of that here. In 1523, Luther advised kindness toward the Jews in *That Jesus Christ was Born a Jew*. He also aimed to convert them to Christianity.

When his efforts at conversion failed, this is the thing that he did. At first he spoke well of Erasmus until Erasmus didn't join him. Once Erasmus didn't join him, he went on the attack. Now he's going to show this same behavior toward the Jewish people.

When his efforts at conversion failed, he grew increasingly bitter toward them. In his 2010 book

Bonhoeffer: Pastor, Martyr, Prophet, Spy, Christian author Eric Metaxas claimed that Luther's attitude toward Jews "unraveled along with his health."

Luther's other major works on the Jews were his 60,000 word treatise *Von den Juden und Ihren Lügen* (*On the Jews and Their Lies*), and *Vom Schem Hamphoras und vom Geschlecht Christi* (*On the Holy Name and the Lineage of Christ*), both published in 1543, three years before his death.

Luther argued that the Jews were no longer the chosen people but "the devil's people," and referred to them with violent, vile language; citing *Deuteronomy* 13. Therein Moses commands the killing of idolaters and the burning of their cities and property as an offering to God. Now imagine what this did. It's:

> "Okay. These haters of God should be burned. They should be killed. Their cities should be burned. Their property should be taken as an offering to God."

Luther called for a "scharfe barmherzigkeit" ("sharp mercy") against the Jews:

> "...to see whether we might save at least a few from the glowing flames."

Luther advocated setting synagogues on fire, destroying Jewish prayer books, forbidding Rabbis from preaching, seizing Jews' property and money and smashing up their homes so that these "envenomed worms" would be forced into labour or expelled "for all time." In Robert Michael's view, Luther's words:

> "We are at fault in not slaying them"

This amounted to a sanction for murder.

> "We are at fault in not slaying them."

Luther says that if we don't kill them, we are guilty!

"God's anger with them is so intense,"

Luther concluded:

"...that gentle mercy will only tend to make them worse, while sharp mercy will reform them but little. Therefore in any case, away with them!"

Luther spoke out against the Jews in Saxony, Brandenburg and Silesia. Josel of Rosheim, the Jewish spokesman who tried to help the Jews of Saxony in 1537, later blamed their plight on:

"...that priest whose name was Martin Luther."

Do you see? He was a priest. Martin Luther was a Catholic priest.

"...May his body and soul be bound up in hell!"

Josel of Rosheim said that Luther wrote and issued many heretical books in which he said that whoever would help the Jews was doomed to perdition. Josel asked the city of Strasbourg to forbid the sale of Luther's anti-Jewish works. They refused initially, but did so when a Lutheran pastor in Hochfelden used a sermon to urge his parishioners to murder Jews. Luther's influence persisted after his death.

Throughout the 1580s, riots led to the expulsion of Jews from several German Lutheran states. Luther was the most widely read author of his generation and within Germany he acquired the status of a prophet.

According to the prevailing view among historians, Luther's anti-Jewish rhetoric significantly contributed to the development of anti-Semitism in Germany and in the

1930s and 1940s provided an "ideal underpinning" for the Nazi's attacks on Jews.

On December 17, 1941, seven Protestant regional church confederations issued a statement agreeing with the policy of forcing Jews to wear the yellow badge. This is all in history.

> "...since after his bitter experience, Luther had already suggested preventive measures against the Jews and their expulsion from German territory."

At the time of the Marburg Colloquy, Suleiman the Magnificent was besieging Vienna with a vast Ottoman army. Luther had argued against resisting the Turks in his 1518 *Explanation of the Ninety-five Theses,* provoking accusations of defeatism.

This is where we're going to see that Luther – well, let me just read this because this is Luther and Islam. He saw the Turks as a scourge sent to punish Christians by God; as agents of the biblical apocalypse that would destroy the Antichrist, **whom Luther believed to be the papacy and the Roman Church.** Luther was the first one to come up with the statement:

> "The Pope is the Antichrist."

When you think about it, there are people today who believe that the Catholic Church is the Antichrist. The Catholic Church is the harlot church and the Pope is the Antichrist. People believe that. Luther was the first one to advocate it. Luther says:

> "Listen, the Islamists – the Muslims have been sent by God"

...and that they were agents of the biblical apocalypse that would destroy the Antichrist. He consistently rejected the idea of a Holy War.

> "...as though our people were an army of Christians against the Turks, who were enemies of Christ. This is absolutely contrary to Christ's doctrine and name."

You will see that same usage today.

"Is America in a Holy War?"

Now listen. Islam – everything that they are doing; all of the terrorists attacks by Muslims, by Islamists, they are attributing it to Mohammed. They believe that they are to establish a caliphate – to reestablish an Islamic caliphate, an empire and the institution of *Sharia* law; which is the Law of God according to the Muslims.

You will find that certain parties or a certain party is trying to urge the leader of this nation to call it a "Holy War" – it is a war against Israel. This stuff is in the news. You have probably heard it. The refusal to call it a "Holy War" simply feeds into the President of the United States as a Muslim. You see, when you have rhetoric that is being spewed, you will find that this strategy goes way back – way back and it is still being used today in a lot of ways.

The people who are not with us must be against us. In order to make us look legitimate, we have to tear everybody else down. Is that what you have to do? Why don't you just preach what you believe to be true? Sometimes in the preaching of what you believe to be true, it exposes people.

It is not that you are trying to expose people. It is that you are preaching what you believe to be true. Anyone who is preaching contrary to what you believe to be true is now being exposed; especially if I am saying one thing and everybody else that they listen to is saying something contrary to that.

"This is what I believe."

And this is what that person believes and on this particular issue, we just don't agree. Can we disagree? Can we disagree without demonizing each other? Can we disagree and still have some kind of relationship? Or if we disagree, do we have to split up over every little disagreement? I will tell you something. You will have what we have today – a very fragmented society.

I don't want to spend a lot more time on Luther, but there is a lot more to spend on Luther. I said that Luther is probably the most influential person in the church world today. All of the teachings and doctrines that we are trying to expose for what they are, were established way back then.

One of the things that I wanted to get to was what Luther had to do in order to get his gospel out. The reason why people translate Bibles is to give you their version. What I did and in Pentecostalism and in the mainline Baptists, there are two Bibles.

There are two Bibles in my walk that have probably been the most influential in churches. At one point, all of the churches that were of a particular denomination were reading from one of these two books. One is the *Thompson Chain Reference Bible.* Anybody ever hear of the Thompson Chain Reference? The other is the *Dakes Bible.* Anybody ever hear of Dakes?

What Dakes did – this is interesting. If you can, you will find that Dakes has commentaries. He has two columns of commentaries; two columns of scriptures into which he also inserts commentaries. He has this big old book with commentary from *Genesis* all the way to *Revelation.* People who read Dakes' Bible read all of his commentaries and preach from these commentaries.

It is the same thing with Thompson's Chain Reference. In the Thompson's Chain Reference Bible, you can see it. You have the words of the Bible and then you have all of the reference material and all of the commentary in the margins. When a person reads the Bible, they read the commentary.

I can't tell you how many times I have found myself having conversations with people who want to argue with me from the commentary of their favorite Bible. Now you have all of these teachers on TV who want to give you their version of the Bible. What they are saying is:

> "Listen. We want to give you an accurate version of a translation of the Bible."

By whose standard? It is going to be bent toward the belief system of that organization. That continues on today, even with the scriptures and the Sacred Name Bibles. People are already encouraging me that I need to write a Bible. I probably will. It's a ways off, but it is probably going to happen to the point where it will have the name and try to replace or to expose some of the things. Or we will make people more aware that as you read the Bible, that here is some misleading information and misinformation.

I mean, think about it ladies and gentlemen. How in the world did "Easter" get into the book? Somebody put it there! And because they put that one word into the book, the church now celebrates "Easter." If you can write your own Bible and put it in the hands of people, then they are going to read your version. All who read your version of the book are going to believe what you put into the book. It is just the way that it is.

Chapter Four

As many of you know, the default response for people when you begin to talk to them about the commands, about the Law and about our responsibility and accountability to the commandments of YeHoVaH, that default verse or statement is:

"Well, what about grace?"

We started this teaching out in *Ephesians* 2:8.

> Eph 2:8-9 – "For by **grace** are ye **saved** through **faith**; and that not of yourselves: *it is* the **gift** of God: ⁹Not of **works**, lest any man should **boast**."

We broke down each of those words. We talked about Martin Luther and his impact on the church as we know it. Many people hear of "Church Fathers" and often times don't know who these Church Fathers are or were. And yet in Bible seminaries and colleges you will hear of *Irenaeus*. You will hear of *Tertullian*. You will hear of *Polycarp* and many of these individuals who have had an impact on the church as we know it today.

But no person has impacted the church as we know it today and the doctrines that people ascribe to, as much as Martin Luther. We began to look at some of the things that Martin Luther did, to try to get an understanding.

We find that the doctrine or theology of grace did not come from Messiah or Paul, but from Luther and Westerners' theological interpretation of Luther, Paul and Messiah. Many of the people that you will deal with; that you will communicate with and debate with and at times even argue with, are arguing from a theological position of a denominational interpretation of Paul's writings and of Yeshua's writings.

Of course they will throw in the early Church Fathers, who basically forged the impression of what the Christian Church is today. The impact of the church as we know it came from individuals outside of the book. The early Church Fathers or the Church Fathers are not found in the book and yet people use the book to validate the Church Fathers' positions.

I will tell you, ladies and gentlemen. You can use this book to validate any position you desire. All you have to do is to misread or misinterpret or take a verse of scripture out of context and make it say what you want. You can string verses together and make them say what you want.

This is why in our Discipleship Training we began to look at all of the principles of interpretation: hermeneutics (the art and science of interpretation) and biblical hermeneutics (the art and science of biblical interpretation).

We did this so that we can rightly divide; so that we can interpret the word the way it was written, versus reading into it. We identified this as *eisegesis,* instead of taking out of it what is there, which is *exegesis*. These are theological terms that we have learned in our Discipleship Training. These will aid us in interpreting the Bible.

Historically three groups emerged outside of Judaism. Those are the Catholics, the Protestants/Lutherans (Catholic Reformers) and of course the Anabaptists. The Anabaptists were part of the Protestants. The Protestants and the Anabaptists basically protested against the Catholic Church. The Catholic Church was doing things in its day. It had a hierarchy and a monopoly on the word to the point where individuals within the Catholic Church identified the fallacy of the papacy and began to address it.

Like any other time in history when you begin to address the leadership of a particular regime, you can find yourself on the outs. In some cases, you can find yourself dead. All an individual has to do is to demonize you, identify you as a heretic and get enough people to believe. Remember that Yeshua was crucified as a heretic. We don't like hearing that, but that is the bottom line.

He was considered to be a blasphemer. What caused him to be crucified was because it was identified that he had blasphemed (according to the scripture). Blaspheming warranted the death penalty. A blasphemer then is a modern day rendition of a heretic. It is someone who is preaching something false.

Yeshua was considered to be a false teacher, a false prophet, a false Messiah, a blasphemer and a heretic. Therefore he was killed, but basically he gave up his life.

The Protestants or Lutherans is what they became known as until religion left Germany. It is amazing that religion or the faith that we know of today as Christianity, started in Rome. It literally started in Jerusalem as they would say. But how many of you know that Jerusalem was under siege by Rome? Rome occupied Israel.

Therefore as Rome occupied Israel, the dominant force was Roman. Rome occupied Israel. Those who were part of Israel were under the control (if you would) and occupation of Rome. It is amazing that Roman Catholicism didn't start in Rome. It started in Israel.

It was an occupation or a religion that had been taken siege by the Romans. As Romans began to confess faith (the Italians/Romans), many of them began to express faith in Messiah. One of the most famous Romans who expressed faith in Messiah is found in the Book of *Acts*. Does anybody know what his name is? Who? Who? Well, Paul was a Roman.

Folks don't know this because they say that Paul was a Benjamite. Paul was a Roman. Paul's citizenship was of Rome. That is how he ended up in Rome, to be tried. But Paul is not who I am talking about, although Paul was a

Roman. He was a Jew or a Benjamite and he was a Roman. But the first Roman that we know of – the centurion? No, it wasn't the centurion. The centurion was in the book, the gospel, the Book of *Acts*. Does anybody know? Come on, no. Cornelius! What else was he? *Romans* chapter number what, ten? *Acts* chapter ten verse 1:

> Acts 10:1 – "There was a certain man in Caesarea called Cornelius, a centurion of the band called the Italian *band*,"

Is that in your Bibles or is it a misprint in mine? What does it say? It was an *Italian* band. He was a man in Caesarea called Cornelius, a centurion. So you are partially right, but you weren't talking about that centurion.

Here we know that many Romans accepted Messiah. It wasn't long before there was dissention. In *Acts* 8 if you remember – we are getting way off course here. In *Acts* 8, there was a persecution. All but the apostles fled Jerusalem. In *Acts* 8:

> Acts 8:1-3 – "Saul was consenting unto his death. At that time there was a great persecution against the assembly which was at Jerusalem, and they were all scattered abroad throughout the region of Judea and Samaria except the apostles."

By the time that Jerusalem fell (if you would); not fell, but the temple was actually destroyed – at this particular time, Judaism as they knew it literally went into disarray. Now the people who were coming up to Jerusalem for worship and for the feasts and festivals were no longer going up to Jerusalem because there was no temple there.

Ultimately Judaism in Jerusalem began to wane. The Messianic faith waned. Then this hybrid brand of what we know of as Catholicism emerged as more and more

Gentiles (non-Jews) began to come into the faith. Now people began to move away from the Hebrew. They began to incorporate the languages of the land, which were Latin and Greek.

At this time, the *Septuagint*, which is the Greek version of the Old Testament Hebrew writings, was already introduced. Well not yet, but it was coming. When it came down to having the Septuagint – I believe it was. I have to do some research on that, but I believe it was. The Septuagint or the Greek version of the Hebrew Bible was already being translated so that individuals in the Hebrew and Greek – the Greek-speaking [people] were able to understand the scriptures. Remember in *Acts* 6?

> Acts 6:1 - "And in those days when the number of the disciples were multiplied, there arose a murmuring of the Greeks."

It was the Grecians against the Hebrews. Now you have some issues going on in the congregation where those who spoke Greek and those who spoke Hebrew begin to complain about one another. These individuals who spoke Greek; their main language was the Greek language. So the question is: how do the Greek-speaking individuals understand the Hebrew Scriptures?

They have to be translated. They have to be interpreted. Do you understand what I am saying? And of course it was the same thing where Latin was the dominant force. The Latin Vulgate became a major part in the translation into the various languages that we know today.

Catholics claim their authority from Peter. Protestants, which is a hybrid or a "mutant" Catholic, claim their authority from Martin Luther. We dealt with Luther as it related to his position with Judaism. We dealt with Luther when it came down to his belief, his faith. And we touched a little bit on Luther and Islam. We're going to continue down that vein. Then we are going to look at Luther and his position concerning a particular book of the Bible.

This is where Luther had some problems. This is what you will find. Because of Luther's influence, people today have problems. People have two major problems which permeate Christianity today. The first is that the predominant Christian community has a dislike for Jewish people. It's just there.

Now there are some, who because of the work of Christian Zionists, have begun to move back into embracing the Jewish people. But for the majority of Christendom, there is still this dislike for the Jewish people. Then the second thing which we all have been confronted with and where it was incorporated into us as a child until our eyes were opened and we began to look for answers, is a dislike or a hatred for "the Law."

Many people hate the Law. Their hatred toward the Law will be taken out on anyone who confesses that we are still under the Law. It is not a matter of grace, ladies and gentlemen. Those who are under Law are also under grace. As a matter of fact, grace is so incorporated into the Law to the point where if it wasn't for grace, none of us would be here – none of us. Father could have destroyed everything and not started over. He could have said:

> "Do you know what? I'm done!"

You know, like some of us. We get "done." We're just too through. He could have done that, and yet the grace and mercy of the Almighty says:

> "You know, if I am asking my people to endure – to have longsuffering..."

He is certainly exercising longsuffering by putting up with the shenanigans of His creation. Right now folks, mankind has gone off the deep end – seriously. I'm just waiting to see what the Supreme Court is going to say to see just how deep that end is.

But Luther on Islam at the time of the Marsburg Colloquy; Suleiman the Magnificent was besieging Vienna with a vast Ottoman army. Luther had argued against resisting the Turks in his 1518 *Explanation of the Ninety-five Theses;* provoking accusations of defeatism.

He saw the Turks as a scourge sent to punish Christians by God; as agents of the biblical apocalypse that would destroy the Antichrist, **whom Luther believed to be the papacy, and the Roman Church.**

You've got folks today who say:

> "Yeah, they're the Anti-Messiah. The Pope is the Anti-Messiah and the Catholic Church is the harlot church."

That idea was first formulated by Luther. He consistently rejected the idea of a Holy War:

> "...As though our people were an army of Christians against the Turks, who were enemies of Christ. This is absolutely contrary to Christ's doctrine and name."

This is what Luther wrote. On the other hand, in keeping with his doctrine of the two kingdoms, Luther did support non-religious war (against the Turks).

Now you have the separation of church and state. You have the state that has vowed to defend itself against all enemies foreign and domestic. An individual can opt-out of military service because of religious values. So a religious person cannot be forced to go to war.

This was part and parcel to the idea that there is the secular and there is the religious. Luther espoused the idea that as a country we have to defend ourselves, but let the heathens do it.

Basically this is what he is saying:

> "Let the people who have no faith fight for the country and the people who are of faith will pray."

This is what he is saying. In 1526, he argued in *Whether Soldiers can be in a state of Grace,* that national defense is reason for a just war. By 1529, in *On War against the Turk,* he was actively urging Emperor Charles V and the German people to fight a secular war against the Turks. He made clear however that the spiritual or holy war against an alien faith was separate; to be waged through prayer and repentance.

This whole idea of calling a nation to prayer and repentence didn't just begin in the United States. You have people today who argue that if we want to see the hand of the Almighty on these good old United States like it was in its founding days of the Founding Fathers of this United States, that the people of the United States have to repent and go back to that old-time religion which was still without the Law.

At no point in American history did America uphold the Law of YeHoVaH! Now individuals will argue that the Constitution of the United States was based in part on the Laws of God. There may be some truth to that. We can certainly see certain Laws on the books in the Constitution. We can find them in the Torah.

But others behind Luther argued based on Luther's writings that the Law should not be in the church, but in the courts. They argued that the only law that man is obligated to is not the Law of God, but the laws of man that are upheld by the court system.

Today what we have is a court system that upholds the laws of the three branches of government: the executive, the judiciary and the legislative. The legislative branch makes the laws. The legislative branch is what? It consists of Congress, the House of Representatives, the Senate and Congressmen. That's the legislative branch. What do they do? They pass bills. These bills that you hear about are laws. These laws are for the governing of the citizens of these United States.

The people who make laws are the legislative branch. The people who enforce the laws are the judicial branch. That is the Supreme Court. That is all of the appellate courts and all of the civil courts, the federal courts, the state courts. And of course the head of state is the executive branch. But interestingly enough you've got the executive branch of government, you've got the legislative branch of government and you've got the judicial branch of government.

This is not only in a federal system, but you've got it in a state system and you've got it in a city system. In a federal government, it's the President, it's the Supreme Court and it's the Congress. In the state government, it's the Governor. The Governor is the head of state.

Then you've got the Supreme Court – the state Supreme Court. Then you've got these individuals – state Senators and Representatives that are sent to the state capitol just as you have within the states, individuals who are sent to the federal capitol in Washington, D.C.

But then on a city level you have the Mayor. You have the Mayor who is the head of the city. You've got the Aldermen and the City Council members. You have the legislative branch. They are making city ordinances. They are determining how deeply to get into the taxpayers' pockets.

They are making laws concerning the streets and concerning the sidewalks and when you sell your property and all of this. You have all of this government stacked on top of one another. If that wasn't enough government, now you have county government that is drawing money and has a responsibility for the state roads and county roads.

You have the sheriffs and the police and the highway patrols. You've got all of this government that has replaced the Laws of God. They have replaced the Laws of YeHoVaH with the laws of men. They uphold the laws of men and decry and denounce the Laws of YeHoVaH.

What you have is a whole other approach to Babel. You have a Babylon system in a whole other model. It is a Nimrod system. That's what it is. You have individuals who are not accountable to any higher power (if you would), but who seek the votes of people who are submitted to this higher power.

Luther says:

> "There is a separation. The church prays and the secular government protects. They go to war. They fight. Our conscience says that the way we wage war is not like the world."

In 1542, Luther read a Latin translation of the Qur'an. He went on to produce several critical pamphlets on Islam, which he called "Mohammedanism" or "the Turk." Although Luther saw the Muslim faith as a tool of the devil, he was indifferent to its practice.

Luther and Faith Alone

Luther was a faith man. He believed in justification by faith and faith alone. When it comes down to faith alone, you have people who take the grace alone approach based on Luther's faith alone view.

Luther published his German translation of the New Testament in 1522. He and his collaborators completed the translation of the Old Testament in 1534, when the whole

Bible was published. He continued to work on refining the translation until the end of his life.

Others had translated the Bible into German, but Luther tailored his own translation to his own doctrine. This has been going on, ladies and gentlemen. The Scofield Bible is the Bible where they introduced the "rapture." People had no knowledge of a rapture until Scofield put in his commentary (in the notes of his Bible), about this "rapture." Folks had never heard of a rapture.

When you listen and you do the research on where he got it from, you would be astounded. But it made its way into the Bible. Now it is predominant in churches around the world! It is the predominant view that one of these good old by and by wakeup mornings, Jesus is going to come and take the church and everybody else will be left behind. They have even made movies. You know it.

When he was criticized for using the word "alone" after "faith" in *Romans* 3:28, this is what he did. I'm going to tell you. Luther made a tailor-made translation of the Bible. He inserted the word "alone" after "faith" in *Romans* 3:28. Have you checked your Bible's *Romans* 3:28?

> Ro 3:28 – "Therefore we conclude that a man is justified by faith [alone] without the deeds of the Law."

Luther inserted "alone." A man is justified by faith alone. Now that simple word, you would say:

> "Why would that make a big difference?"

Guess what? There is a word in the Bible that has made so much of a difference in the lives of individuals that an entire holy day has been incorporated around it – Easter. One word inserted into the Bible has had a profound impact on the faith that claims its existence from the Bible. So in simply adding one word, you change the meaning. This is why YeHoVaH says:

> "You will not add to it nor will you diminish from it. You don't add one thing to it, you don't take anything away from it because the moment you add something to it, you change the entire structure – the foundation. You've destroyed it simply by adding a word."

Luther did this. Somebody caught him. I will tell you, it had to be some very insightful individuals to find one word. I mean out of all of the Bibles, out of all the words that Luther wrote, they are scrutinizing his work so much that they said:

> "Okay, he added this word 'alone.'"

This is his argument.

> "[T]he text itself and its meaning of St. Paul urgently require and demand it."

He says that if you look at what Paul meant and what he said, it requires that word being put there.

> "...For in that very passage he is dealing with the main point of Christian doctrine; namely that we are justified by faith in Christ without any works of the Law."

So based on his interpretation, he said that it is justified. But when works are so completely cut away, that must mean that faith alone justifies. Do you see what he is doing? He is using deduction – the science of deduction. We're going to make this argument which, if you listen to me long enough, I'm going to lead you to my conclusion.

He says but when works are so completely cut away, if we remove works, then it *must mean* that faith alone justifies. Whoever would speak plainly and clearly about this cutting away of works would have to say that faith alone justifies us and not works. That's his argument.

Published at a time of rising demand for German language publications, Luther's version quickly became a popular and influential Bible translation. As such, it made a significant contribution to the evolution of the German language and literature.

If you think that this is interesting, wait until you do the research on how the English language came to be. It is a mixture. It is such a mixture of languages. When it comes down to translations, I have to hand it to him. Luther was a bright, brilliant individual. He knew that he had the ability to influence. At the time, he was more influential than the Pope himself!

After all, the Pope was the head of the Catholic Church. Luther had protested and had a complete following who were now getting away from the Catholic Church. They didn't really like the Catholic Church because of all of the indulges and the elaborate lifestyles that they were living while the people were in abject poverty.

Luther became a figure with a following. He was the head of a movement. Whenever there is a head of a new movement, typically there is a need to write a new translation, a new version and to make new rules and regulations as to how it is to be governed. This is what Paul was doing when he wrote his letter.

You see, Paul wrote letters to an emerging congregation of people who had never practiced this faith before. You have individuals who were coming out of Judaism. All they knew was Judaism. They were coming into a faith that was saying that Judaism is tradition and tradition makes the word of no effect. They were leaving traditions.

You had people who were coming out of different religious backgrounds or non-religious backgrounds. They were coming together in a congregational setting like this. Now you have to bring some order and some structure. The

Bible becomes a blueprint if you would, on how you do that. While Paul was using the Bible[1] as a blueprint to bring this order and to bring this structure, people said:

> "Well, if Paul is using the Bible, then his letters are filled with Bible, so it must be inspired; therefore it has a place in the Bible."

Folks, when we begin to look behind a lot of this, most individuals – 97-98% of people of faith aren't even interested in all of this stuff. I mean, if it's not in the Bible, what difference does it make? Whether you know it or not, it is in the Bible.

The influence of these individuals upon the Bible found its way into the Bible. It began to forge and mold the thinking of religious people. This is why when you are dealing with people; you will find that they are not arguing from the Bible. They are arguing from doctrine – doctrines that the Bible actually refutes.

In order for people to argue their doctrines, they are left with no choice but to cut and paste. They are going to go from verse to verse or from one passage to another and take verses way out of context.

Furnished with notes and prefaces by Luther and with woodcuts by Lucas Cranach that contained anti-papal imagery, it played a major role in the spread of Luther's doctrine throughout Germany. This was his translation of the Bible.

I let you all in on a couple of translations. Here is one that you all may not know of. Anybody ever heard of the Hebrew/Gentile/Israelite scriptures? The Hebrew/Gentile/

---

[1] All use of the word "Bible" here with respect to Paul actually refers to the books of the *Tanakh* (the five books of "Moses" and the writings and the prophets), since the canon of the Bible wasn't officially assembled until centuries later.

Israelite scripture has its translation for its groups of people.

(Arthur grabs another book and holds it up.) This book is the most influential in many of the mainline and specifically the "Word" Churches. In the Word Churches it's the Thompson Chain Reference Bible. And in many of the Pentecostals, especially the Holiness Pentecostals, it is the Dake's Annotated Bible.

As I shared with you all, in several of these Bibles, you will find that you have notes and chain references on the inside and outside. These are leading. Basically it says in these references that if you want to cross-reference this verse, go here. If I am a Baptist, then the chain reference is going to take you to my pet verses related to this. People see the verse reference. Some people say:

> "Oh, there is a verse reference there, so that means that this must be true."

It is amazing. A number of times I have checked out the verse reference and it has absolutely nothing to do with the verse that it is referencing!

Then of course this one has notes galore. I mean it is full of notes. They are even incorporated into the actual passages. If you are a person who believes that every word in this book is God's word from *Genesis* to *Revelation,* then guess what? Even the commentary is the "word" of God. This is what people say:

> "This is my Bible. I believe it is the word of God. It's the unadulterated, infallible word. You can't argue with it from *Genesis* to *Revelation.* It is His word."

What better place to get your belief systems across than by putting it in your version of the Bible? Now you begin to control the minds, the thinking, the reading and the understanding of the people. After all, this is the only version that they use.

You know, it saddens me to some degree. We constantly get people saying:

> "You know, what version of the Bible do you read from? What's the best version of the Bible? Is there a version of the Bible that has the names the way that the names should be?"

I'll tell you. If that version came out, people would get that and who would believe that. That would become their only source. You should never rely upon any one source – never. I don't care who put it out.

The Luther Bible influenced other vernacular translations, such as William Tyndale's English Bible (1525 forward). It was a precursor of the King James Bible.

Luther and the Book of *James* – this is where it gets interesting. Martin Luther denied that the Book of *James* was the work of an apostle. He termed it an "epistle of straw" as compared to some other books in the New Testament. He did this not in the least because of the conflict he thought it rose with Paul on the doctrine of justification.

You see, when you move on a position of faith alone, then *James* is going to mess with you. *James* is saying:

> "Wait a minute. Show me your faith. I'll show you my works."

Luther read *James* and said:

> "Wait a minute. This doesn't belong in the Bible."

Why? Because it conflicted with his beliefs. This is the challenge that people will have. I'm going to tell you something. When I was a Baptist, the predominant gospel of the Baptist Church was the book of *Matthew*. This is where the formula comes from that:

> "You shall baptize in the name of the Father, the Son and the Holy Spirit."

It's the only book in the New Testament that has that formula. They argue to the death that it has to be done this way. Do you follow me?

So the Baptists – John the Baptist – the formula for baptism and with all of that, *Matthew* is the predominant gospel. When you have a predominant gospel, then what is going to happen is that you are going to find yourself coming away with a belief system. That is just like so many who believe that Yeshua celebrated the Passover with his disciples.

If you depend upon a particular version of the Bible or a particular gospel or a particular book, then you will build your doctrine upon that; and if you don't compare them. This is why in theological circles they have what is called *Synoptic Gospels*. You have to fuse all of these gospels together to get a fuller picture of the gospel accounts.

I was exposed to the idea that in order to justify your position, you now have to discredit the positions of others. This is where I was first introduced to the idea of discrediting *Mark* and *Luke*. When you look at the disciples of Yeshua, where do Mark and Luke fit in?

How is it that Mark can write a gospel when Mark was not a disciple? How can Luke write a gospel when Luke was not a disciple? Do you see? You can begin to make your arguments based on the fact that Luke and Mark now have to get someone to tell them what happened. Matthew and John were eyewitnesses. Do you follow me?

In a classroom setting in a Bible College or in a Seminary like any other institute of higher learning, the professor is the professional. The students are learning from the professional professors. The professors are literally discipling. Their classroom is a discipleship center. They are shaping and forging the minds and mentalities of future pastors.

Here you are as a professor in a particular university; teaching students year after year after year. They have to go through your system. They have to pass. If you are the professor of theology in this institution, any person who is going through a theology major is going to spend a lot of time in your classroom under your tutelage where you are their professor. They are going to come out quoting you. They are going to come out believing like you believe.

So if you are a student of Luther, if Luther has an issue with *James*, then guess what? You are going to have an issue with *James*. If Luther has an issue with tongues, guess what? You're going to have an issue with tongues. If Luther has an issue with whatever Luther has an issue with, his followers are going to have issues with the same.

If you are a Baptist student, you are going to think like a Baptist. You are going to read the Bible like a Baptist. You are going to pray like a Baptist. You are going to preach like a Baptist. You are going to act like one. That is because you have been *indoctrinated*.

> James 2:1 – "My brethren, have not the faith of our Lord Yeshua Messiah, *the Lord* of glory, with **respect of persons."**

We are going to look at *James*. We are going to go through it. This is going to be an expository (if you would); an exposition of *James* 2. *James* 2 is filled with so many nuggets. There is so much information that we can spend quite a bit of time right here.

We talked about the work. The question came up just last Sabbath concerning the respect of persons. James deals with that issue. The word he uses there is *prosopolepteo* meaning: "o respect the person (i.e. the external condition of man); to have respect of persons, [basically to] **discriminate**."

What James is doing is that James is not coming up with something. James is coming from the Torah. We are going to see that when James talks about the Law of Liberty, he is saying that you will find it in the Law. Freedom is in the Law. Christians interpret the Law of Liberty as some law that is liberty without even knowing what law they are even referring to.

"Well, it's the Law of Liberty."

Okay, well where is the Law of Liberty? Explain the Law of Liberty. The Law of Liberty is the Torah. The Torah is freedom. The Torah is liberty. The Torah is freedom. Yeshua came to show us and to set the captives free. How? By taking them away from the traditions of men and calling them back to the Torah of YeHoVaH.

YeHoVaH took a people who were in captivity who had a slave mentality, to bring them into freedom and to give them the Law of YeHoVaH that will keep them free. When they neglected the Law of YeHoVaH, what happened? They went back into bondage.

Contrary to popular belief, not being under the Law puts you into bondage. *The Law is freedom.* Why? Because whom the Son sets free, is free indeed. When he came to set the captives free, who did he come to? He came to his own who had been captive – Judaism. They were in bondage to the traditions of men and to the manmade rules and regulations.

They were under the control of the Rabbis, the religious leaders, the Ravs. Now you have people who want to be under the control of the Rabbis. It's the same mindset. We want a Rabbi. We want a Rabbi. Yeshua says:

"Call no man 'Rabbi.'"

The fact that a person wants a Rabbi is an indication that they have rejected *the* Rabbi. He says:

> "You only have one. Just one."

Word usage: To judge based on outward appearances. Now where James gets this from is from *Leviticus*. *Leviticus* says:

> Lev 19:15 – "Ye shall do no unrighteousness in judgment: thou shalt not **respect the person** of the poor, nor honour the person of the mighty: *but* in righteousness shalt thou judge thy neighbour."

In other words, every one of you should be judged by the same merit. You shouldn't judge a woman (because she's a woman) with a different judgment of a man. A lawbreaker is a lawbreaker, regardless of the gender, regardless of the ethnicity and regardless of the economic status. Whether you are a poor lawbreaker or a rich lawbreaker, you are still a lawbreaker. The Almighty says:

> "Don't respect a person because of their poverty."

That is because sometimes people have compassion for the underdog. They have compassion for the poor. But if the poor break the Law of YeHoVaH, they are going to suffer the same fate as the wealthy. Do you understand? YeHoVaH says:

> "Do not do that. Don't judge based on economic status. Don't let somebody off because..."

James goes as far as to say:

> Jas 2:2 – "For if there come unto your assembly a man..."

Here is where he takes this from *Leviticus* 19, because YeHoVaH says:

> "Don't judge because of a poor person. Don't respect a poor person. Don't respect a rich person."

> Lev 19:15 – "...*but* in righteousness shalt thou judge they neighbour."

You judge the poor person with the same righteousness that you would judge the rich person. Don't discriminate. James goes as far as to say:

> Jas 2:2 – "For if there come unto your assembly a man with a gold ring, in goodly apparel, and there come in also a poor man in vile raiment;"

Now do you see what is going on here? One is going to be treated differently "because."

> Jas 2:3 – "And ye have respect to him that weareth the gay clothing,"

You see, this is when "gay" was popular not the "gay" as we know it today. In other words, they have colorful, wealthy, well to do clothing.

> "...and say unto him, 'Sit thou here' in a good place; and say to the poor, 'Stand thou there, or sit here under my footstool:'"

> Jas 2:4 – "Are ye not then partial..."

Now you are showing partiality.

> "...in yourselves, and are become judges of evil thoughts?"

This is where respect of persons comes from. Every one of us starts off at the same place – your relationship with the Almighty and my relationship with the Almighty. When you do what is required of you; within the word itself there are blessings and curses. When you obey the word, you will experience the blessings. When you disobey the word, you will experience the curses.

It's not that YeHoVaH has favor or lack of favor with you. It is that you are doing what is required to enter into the place of blessings; or neglecting the things that are causing the curses.

It is a righteous judgment. The good news is that if a person is in a place where they have brought curses upon themselves, they can repent. The bad news is that if a person is in a place where they are bringing blessings upon themselves, they can repent. You can say:

> "Do you know what? I don't like all of this favor. Give me some curses!"

Just walk away!

> Jas 2:5 – "Hearken my beloved brethren, Hath not God chosen the poor of this world rich in faith, and heirs of the kingdom which he hath promised to them that love him?"

> Jas 2:6 – "But ye have despised the poor. Do not rich men oppress you, and draw you before the judgment seats?"

> Jas 2:7 – "Do not they blaspheme that worthy name by which ye are called?"

Then James goes off and says something like this. Now "he" is really messing with Luther here.

> Jas 2:8 – "If ye fulfil the **royal law** according to the scripture,"

What scripture? He is saying:

> "Listen, there is a Royal Law and the Royal Law is in the scripture."

> "...Thou shalt love thy neighbor as thyself, ye do well:"

He tells us what the Law is – what the Royal Law is. Now he is saying that the Law has some royalty associated with it. The Law of Love is *Leviticus* 19:18. It is called the "Royal Law" because it is the Supreme Law that is the source of all other Laws governing human relationships.

> Lev 19:18 – "Thou shalt not avenge, nor bear any grudge against the children of thy people, but thou shalt love thy neighbor as thyself: I *am* YeHoVaH."

This is where that Law comes from. People say:

> "Brother, if you loved the Lord your God with all of your heart..."

Do you know that is the Law? The second one is:

> "Love your neighbor as yourself."

That's the Law! If you are going to keep some aspect of the Law and not keep all of it, why even mess with it? A person will even go so far as to say:

> "If you break one, you break them all."

Well, if you keep one, you are supposed to be keeping them all! Make up your mind. Either you are under it, or you are not!

> "Well now brother, you are confusing me."

> "No, you are already confused! I'm trying to unconfuse you."

> Mt 22:36 – "Master, which *is* the great commandment in the law?"

Everybody wants to know. His disciples know. Yeshua doesn't say:

> "Well, we're not under the Law. We're under grace. Don't worry about it."

No, he says unto them:

> Mt 22:37 – "Yeshua said unto him, 'Thou shalt love the Lord they Elohim with all thy heart, and with all thy soul, and with all thy mind.'"

> Mt 22:38 – "This is the first and great commandment."

> Mt 22:39 – "And the second *is* like unto it, Thou shalt love they neighbour as thyself."

> Mt 22:40 – "On these two commandments hang all the law and the prophets."

How? Now you have people who want to say:

> "Well, the first commandment is to love the Lord. The second portion of the Ten Commandments is to love God. That's all we are responsible for – the ten."

It's like:

> "You know, that sounds really pretty. It does."

Bu that is not what he is saying. James goes as far as to say:

> Jas 2:9 – "**But if ye have respect to persons,** ye commit sin,"

Now wait a minute.

> "...and are <u>convinced of the law as transgressors</u>."

So a New Testament person who has respect of persons, has transgressed the Law. Why? Because in the Law it says that you should not do that.

> Jas 2:10 – "For <u>whosoever shall keep the whole law,</u> and <u>yet offend in one *point*, he is guilty of all</u>."

We're going to break that down for you. James is not saying:

> "Listen. If you break one Law, you've broken them all, so don't worry about them. Don't do any of them. If you don't do any of them, you have broken them all too."

But people take it and say:

> "See? If you break one, you've broken all of them."

Okay, now what? So what do you do? If you have broken one, you have broken all of them. What are you saying to me? That I don't have to do any of them? James already said:

> "Listen. There is a Royal Law."

Do you get it? There's a Royal Law, so you have to do something. If you don't do this, you have transgressed the Law. But if you break one, you have broken all of them, and yet you have to keep something in the Law.

> "But what about grace, brother?"

Grace is "all up in here." I will leave you with this:

Jas 2:11 – "For he that said, 'Do not commit adultery,' said also, 'Do not kill.' Now if thou commit no adultery, yet if thou kill, thou art become a transgressor of the law."

Jas 2:12 – "So speak ye, and so do, as they that shall be judged by the law of liberty."

James speaks about this Law of Liberty more than once. We are going to look at this next. We still have to get to Luther and faith. Hallelujah.

Chapter Five

I'm planning on concluding the message that we have been dealing with on *What About Grace?* We are looking at some of the teachings that are out there and topics that we run across when dealing with individuals when sharing our faith and what we believe; especially as we are talking to individuals who are part of the world that we have left. What I mean by the world that we have left is that many of us have been in different churches. We have established relationships with different people in churches.

As we have taken upon ourselves to literally see what the Bible actually teaches versus just sucking in the teachings that we have been taught, we have come to realize that there are disconnects between what we have been taught and what the Bible actually teaches.

We started this particular *Searching the Scriptures* series dealing with a message that was about Yeshua having a conversation with the Pharisees. We know that the Pharisees were the religious leaders and teachers. As the Bible opens up in the New Testament, we know that there was religion that had already been established among the Jewish believers, if you would.

There were two schools that we know of from the scripture. Those were the Pharisees and the Sadducees. We have learned from extra biblical material that there was also a group called the Essenes. We know that Yeshua specifically addressed the belief systems pertaining to the Pharisees, the Sadducees and Herod.

We acknowledged that the Pharisees were those who were responsible for leading the synagogue worship. The Sadducees were those who were responsible for leading the temple worship. Then there were those who followed

Herod, who was the king. Although he was not chosen by YeHoVaH, he certainly was the king of Israel. There were those who followed Herod; which represents the government.

Yeshua was basically saying to beware of the teachings of those who lead the synagogue worship. Beware of the teachings of those who lead the temple worship and beware of the teachings of the government. In our day, we deal with Republicans and Democrats. People take sides. They begin to apply the Bible; even to their political ambitions.

As Yeshua began to address some of the issues of his day, in confronting the Pharisees he said:

> "Search the scriptures, for therein you *think* you have eternal life. Search the scriptures, for therein you *think* you have eternal life."

In stating that, he is saying to these religious leaders who were supposedly teaching the commands of YeHoVaH that they were literally teaching something else. Those who followed the commands of YeHoVaH knew that there was one who would come. This one, who would come, would be the Messiah King. This would be the King of Israel and the Messiah whom YeHoVaH would send and who would teach Israel the things that they need to know.

We know that the woman at the well actually made the statement that:

> "We know that Messiah comes. And when he comes, he will tell us all things."

The religious leaders of Yeshua's day were supposedly looking for the Messiah. However when the Messiah showed up, they didn't recognize him. The reason why they didn't recognize him was because they weren't teaching the Torah. They were teaching the traditions and the laws of men. Therefore as they were teaching the laws and the traditions of men, they had abandoned the Law of God. Had they stayed with the Law of God, they would have recognized the Messiah.

We started this journey in *Searching the Scriptures* with that foundation in mind. Now we have evolved into the statement of defense. The statement of defense that typically comes up when a person is cornered and you have eradicated their arguments; their default statement is:

"What about grace? What about grace?"

We wanted to tackle that particular subject. About four weeks ago [as Arthur teaches this], actually five weeks ago [this is week five], we began that journey in dealing with *What About Grace?* We hope to conclude that so that we can go on to *Faith.* That will more than likely be the next series that we deal with because it is important for believers to understand faith. The Bible teaches that for without faith, it is impossible to please YeHoVaH.

(There is a short lapse in video footage and teaching resumes in progress.)

Praise Him. Did you all miss us? For a brief moment there ladies and gentlemen, we were "covered." Now we have been unveiled again. Hallelujah.

Today we're going to be talking about grace in the teaching *What About Grace?* This teaching's foundation is in *Ephesians* 2:8:

> Eph 2:8-9 – "For by **grace** are ye **saved** through **faith**; and that not of yourselves: *it is* the **gift** of God: ⁹Not of **works**, lest any man should **boast**."

As we noted, the doctrine or theology of grace did not come from Messiah or Paul, but from Luther and Westerners' theological interpretation of Luther, Paul and Messiah.

In the last chapter and the chapter before last, we began to look at some of Luther. In the last chapter specifically, we went in-depth into some of the things that Luther taught. We also pointed out that historically speaking three groups emerged outside of Judaism. They were the Catholics, Protestants or Lutherans, which are Catholic Reformers. Luther was a Catholic all of his life. Then of course there were those that were the offshoots of Protestantism; which are the Anabaptists.

They actually teach that a person had to be baptized as an adult once they had the ability to know the decision that they were making. They also taught that infant baptism was not biblical.

You have to understand something. Being baptized as a child is not unbiblical, but there seems to be that indication because John came and baptized individuals. We don't know if John baptized children. We don't know. We don't know if John baptized mothers with babies. We don't, but we assume so. We don't see every one that John baptized.

I don't necessarily agree with infant baptism. But what I am saying is that anyone that wanted to make an argument that you must be able to acknowledge your faith and base that teaching on the Bible, now also has to reconcile what Paul was talking about as far as fathers, moms and dads, or husbands and wives not divorcing one another because of the children – the children being sanctified or the children being clean.

I'm not here trying to make an argument for infant baptism. What I am saying is that the Anabaptists made an argument that being baptized as a child was not biblical.

Catholics claim their authority from Peter. Protestants are a hybrid or a "mutant" Catholic. They claim their authority from Martin Luther. Martin Luther had some big problems. The biggest problem Martin Luther had was with the Book of *James. James* was a problem for Martin Luther.

> Jas 2:9 – "But if ye have respect to persons, ye commit sin, and are convinced of the law as transgressors."

We looked at this, but I didn't bring any depth to it. I want to do so here.

> Jas 2:10 – "**For whoosoever <u>shall keep the whole law, and yet offend in one *point*, he is guilty of all.</u>**"

How many of you have had that thrown at you as you talked about keeping the commands?

> "Well, if you break one Law brother, you've broken them all!"

It is unfortunate that some use this passage as a means to reject the Law. They say:

> "It is impossible to keep the Law because if you break one, you break them all."

Well, that is true when you think about the fact that if you add one letter to the Torah, you have now destroyed the Torah. If you take one letter away from it; if you add one word or if you take one word away from it, you have now destroyed it.

So if you break one of the Laws, then you are now a lawbreaker. Does that mean that because you broke one Law, that now you are incapable of keeping any of the Law? It doesn't mean that, but that is how it is interpreted. The argument is that if you break one Law, you break them all. Therefore the logic is that since you cannot keep the Law, what is the point of trying?

You can go along with that logic and blow the logic out of the water and say:

> "Okay, so it's okay to commit adultery."

"Well, no brother, it's not."

"Well, what's the point? If I broke one Law, I've broken them all. So you are saying that I can't keep any of it. I'm not capable of keeping it."

Let's take this even further. The message communicated is that it is impossible to keep the Law. There is no way one can keep the commandments (they say). The commandments are "too hard" to keep. You "can't" keep them all, so why bother trying to keep any of the commandments of the Law?

If you take that logic at face value, you come to the conclusion that God gave the people commandments that He knew they could not keep. This is where the logic leads to. However, the Bible tells us that the Law or the commandments are not burdensome or too hard to keep. This is what the Bible teaches. Now, what your pastor teaches, what your Bishop and Elders teach; that is something else.

But here is what the Bible teaches. Just as if you break one Law, it makes it difficult to keep the Law, then we should not keep any Law. That is because to keep any of the commandments would be an attempt to keep a commandment. Think about it. If I try to keep *any* commandment, that would be an attempt to keep the Law. So why am I trying to keep any commandment?

Does this make sense to you? If I can't keep any of them, why attempt to keep any of them? The fact that I'm trying to keep any commands like *Honor Your Father and Mother* – you won't find a Christian out there who is not under the burden of honoring or trying to honor their Father and Mother.

This one really gets me. These Charismatic Pentecostals came up with the idea to justify the illicit or the ungodly lifestyle of their pastors when they made this statement:

> "Touch not my anointed and do my prophet no harm."

Now wait a minute, hold it, hold it, hold it. That comes straight out of the Law. That is straight out of the Law! You see, if I had my computer – my computer, this is not mine. I'd find that verse. Somebody find it for me, if you can.

> "Touch not my anointed."

Or:

> "Do my prophet no harm."

Those are key words you can search.

YeHoVaH's Law was not too hard to keep or burdensome or too heavy. Here is what it says in 1 *John:*

> 1 Jo 5:3 – "For this is the love of God, that we keep his commandments: and his commandments are not **grievous**."

Yes. 1 *Chronicles?* Okay. Now it's 1 *Chronicles* 16:15-22. Now look at what it is referring to. Verse 15:

> 1 Chron 16:15 – "Remember the covenant which he first commanded to a thousand generations,"

Where is that at? *Exodus* chapter 20.

> 1 Chron 16:16 – "the covenant which he made with Abraham,"

Where is Abraham at? *Genesis* chapter 12.

> 1 Chron 16:17 – "He also confirmed it to Jacob"

Where is Jacob? *Genesis.*

> 1 Chron 16:17 – "For a statute to Israel as an everlasting covenant"

Jacob became the twelve tribes of Israel. Where did that happen? In the Law.

> 1 Chron 16:18 – "Saying to you I will give the land of Canaan and as the portion of your inheritance."

> 1 Chron 16:19 – "When they were only few in number, very few and strangers in it"

> 1 Chron 16:20 – "and they wandered about from nation to nation..."

This is the forty years in the wilderness.

> 1 Chron 16:20 – "...from one kingdom to another people."

> 1 Chron 16:21 – "He permitted no man to oppress them; and he reproved kings for their sakes saying:"

He reproved kings for their sake, so that says to me that there should be a reference to this somewhere in the Torah. He reproved kings for their sake, saying:

> 1 Chron 16:22 – "Touch not my anointed ones; and do my prophets no harm."

Now, who are the anointed ones? Who? Who? Israel was the anointed ones. Who was the prophet? Abraham was a prophet. Moses was a prophet. There were many in the Torah who prophesied. In the Torah, do you remember the seventy elders? They all prophesied. Two were in the camp. They were Eldad and Medad. They prophesied in the camp. So He says to the kings during the sojourning in the wilderness:

> "Touch not my prophet. Touch not my anointed."

And people want to associate this to their Bishop.

> "Touch not my anointed."

The Bishop is not the anointed. It's the people that the Bishop is supposed to be "Bishop-ing" over. THEY are the anointed. YOU are the anointed! So you have people who are *taking scriptures way out of context* and twisting them in order to sanctify the ungodly living of their pastors that they are trying to protect.

His commandments are not grievous. This is the love of God. If you love Him, what are you going to try to do? Keep His commandments! You are not going to be saying:

> "We're not under the Law! You can't keep the commandments!"

If you can't keep the commandments, you can't love God! If you are not trying to keep the commandments, you don't love Him. This IS the love of God; that we keep His commandments and His commandments are not grievous!

The word here *barus* means: "heavy in weight; a metaphor; burdensome; severe; stern; weighty; of great moment; violent, cruel, unsparing." The word *grievous* here means heavy.

That is a good word for it. Now the reason why I point out this word "heavy," is because you will find that this word heavy is also *barus.* Here the laws instituted by the Pharisees and the Sadducees were heavy. They were barus. They were burdensome. This is what it says.

> Mt 23:2 – "Saying, the scribes and the Pharisees sit in Moses' seat:"
>
> Mt 23:3 – "All therefore whatsoever they bid you observe, *that* observe and do; but do not ye after their works: for they say, and do not."
>
> Mt 23:4 – "For they bind **heavy burdens** and grievous to be borne, and lay *them* on men's shoulders; but they *themselves* will not move them with one of their fingers."

YeHoVaH's Law is not grievous. YeHoVaH's Law is not burdensome. It is the laws of the Pharisees and the Sadducees that were burdensome and grievous. People confuse the two. They think that because the Pharisees and the Sadducees were the representatives of God and the teachers of Israel, they were keeping the Law when they weren't keeping the Law.

They weren't teaching the Law. They were teaching their commandments. They were teaching their traditions. Their traditions and their laws were burdensome and grievous. They lay upon men's shoulders, but they themselves would not move them with one finger. That is what Yeshua says.

> Mt 23:4 – "For they bind **heavy burdens** and grievous to be borne, and lay *them* on men's shoulders; but they *themselves* will not move them with one of their fingers."

In other words, they are telling you to do something that they themselves are not doing.

The same word heavy, burden, is the same word *barus*. YeHoVaH's Law is not barus. The Pharisees' laws are.

Denominational laws may be, but YeHoVaH's Laws are not. They are not too heavy.

> Mt 23:5 – "But all their works they do for to be seen of men: they make broad their phylacteries, and enlarge the borders of their garments,"

Do you know what that means? They have tzitzits down to their ankles. They want you to know, you see. It is interesting that a person can enlarge the borders of their garments and not see tzitzits, unless you know about tzitzits. No, they are not wearing oversized clothes.

> Mt 23:6 – "And love the uppermost rooms at feasts, and the chief seats in the synagogues,"

This is why a lot of pastors are trying to get lovey-dovey with politicians; so they can get invited to the dinners. They can get invited to the State House. They want the Governor to know them. They want to be able to go and sing at the White House. They love the chief seats. They want to look and feel important.

> Mt 23:7 – "And greetings in the markets, and to be called of men 'Rabbi, Rabbi.'"

> Mt 23:8 – "But be not ye called 'Rabbi:' for one is your Master, *even* Messiah; and all ye are brethren."

It is interesting when people come here and say:

"Well, what do we call you?"

I know when I was in the church; at first I liked "Reverend." Reverend sounded holy. Then it was "Elder." You see, when people call you Reverend, it means that they hold you in esteem. You could tell when a person stopped holding you in esteem, because they stopped calling you Reverend. They started calling you by your first name. It is like you go from Elder to Arthur. Yeah. So people asked me:

"What do we call you?"

I said:

"Arthur."

You know? First of all, if you don't put me on a pedestal, you can't take me down. Hallelujah!

Back to *James:*

> Jas 2:11 – "For he that said, 'Do not commit adultery,' said also,"

So if you break one Law, you break them all. He says:

> Jas 2:11 – "...also, 'Do not kill.' Now if thou commit no adultery, yet if thou kill, thou art become a transgressor of the law."

What he is trying to make the case for is, listen. What is really interesting (and we will go into some of this some other time), is who is James talking to? I will give you a precursor right now. Remember those of you who have gone through Discipleship Training, the first thing that you want to know when a book is written is who wrote it? Who did they write it to, and why? James tells us quickly.

> Jas 1:1 – "James, a bondservant of God and of Yeshua Messiah,"

To who? To who? Do you mean the twelve "Christians?" You've got to mean the twelve "Christians," not the twelve tribes. Hmm? What does it say in your Bible? What does it say? Who has "twelve tribes" in theirs? Let me see your hands. What do you have? You're not there yet? What do you have, mama? Hmm? *James* chapter one. Twelve tribes? Twelve tribes? Twelve tribes? So it is in all of your Bibles?

The twelve tribes what? Which were scattered. Now wait a minute. It says the twelve tribes which were scattered. How can the twelve tribes be scattered when they are lost? And when were they scattered and where were they scattered from? (Laughs)

Now James seems to know that the twelve tribes, where they were scattered, were going to get an opportunity to read this letter, because that is who he is writing to! For some reason James is under the impression that the twelve tribes are not lost! Oh, ladies and gentlemen, we miss so much sometimes by ignoring chapter one verses one and two. (Laughs) Do you understand what I am saying?

James knows exactly who he is writing to. Guess what? If you are not part of the twelve tribes, then it may be a little challenging for you to understand what James is writing. James has a specific argument or a specific audience who would understand James' argument. Now, this is important as we look at *What About Grace?*

> Jas 2:11 – "For he that said, 'Do not commit adultery,' said also, 'Do not kill.' Now if thou commit no adultery, yet if thou kill, thou art become a transgressor of the law."

> Jas 2:12 – "So speak ye, and so do, as they that shall be judged by..."

What?

> "...the **law of liberty**."

Understand that the twelve tribes would understand and know the Law. James refers to the Law as a **Law of Liberty;** and not just once. *James* 1:25 – Look at what he says:

> Jas 1:25 – "But whoso looketh into the perfect **law of liberty**, and continueth *therein,* he being not a forgetful hearer, but a doer of the work, this man shall be blessed in his deed."

This Law of Liberty is perfect. How many Laws are there in James' day? How many Christians are there? None! So you can't Christianize *James*. James is speaking specifically to people who know the Law. These are people who understand the Law. They understand that the Law is not bondage; that it is not burdensome. The Law is *freedom.*

That is what distinguished Israel from every other nation. It was a nation that had been delivered from tyranny, delivered from oppression, delivered from bondage and set free by the Almighty Himself. He says:

> "Listen. No other nation on the planet is going to have the Laws that you have. I'm going to distinguish you from everybody else. I'm going to exalt you above all the other nations of the earth. Here is what is going to keep you separate. Here is what is going to keep you number one."

> "Here is what is going to keep you exalted above all the other nations of the earth. If you hearken to diligently keep all these commandments that I'm giving you today, all of these blessings will come upon you in abundance."

> "You will never be in bondage again. You will always be a lender. You will never have to be a borrower. You will always be on top.

You will never be underneath. You will be blessed in the city, blessed in the country. You will be blessed in whatever you put your hands to."

Now you have people out there who are telling you that the Law is "cursed"?

> **How can you curse what YeHoVaH has blessed? You can't do it!**

For those of you half-stepping, jaw-jerking, Torah wanna-be's – you have people who are saying:

"Torah, Torah, Torah."

Man, you have folks who are walking around here talking about:

"Torah, Torah, Torah."

They won't even wear tzitzits! I'm watching these guys at these conferences. You know, you want to look all Jewish and you have your microtallit on and you want to pray prayers. Then you take that microtallit off and you don't even have tzitzits on. I'm watching them as they are going to their cars and going through the airports.

"Where's your tzitzits brother? You're a Torah teacher!"

"You want to talk Torah? Let's talk Torah. I'll show you I'm an observer of Torah."

Do you hear what I'm saying? These tzitzits are for the purpose so that you won't forget! The fact that I'm not wearing them is an indication that I have already forgotten. He said:

"Now wear these, so that you remember."

What do I need to remember them for? When I'm in the Assembly? All of the time. I especially need to remember them when I am not in the Assembly. It is easy for me to try to live and walk in Torah in the midst of the Assembly. But when I leave the Assembly, that's when the challenge comes; when I'm among heathens and surrounded by worldly people.

You want to talk Torah and you want to carry the Torah and touch the Torah and kiss the Torah. Why don't you *live* the Torah? That's what I'm saying. Live it!

> Jas 1:25 – "But whoso looketh into the perfect **law of liberty**, and continueth *therein,* he being not a forgetful hearer, but a doer of the work, this man shall be blessed in his deed."

What work? The Torah requires work! I have to work at not doing things and I have to work at doing things. I have to work at keeping the commandments, because it's easier not to. Do you understand what I am saying?

> Jas 1:25 – "...he being not a forgetful hearer, but a doer of the work, this man shall be blessed in his deed."

What is James saying? If you keep the Torah; if you look into this perfect Law of Liberty and you continue therein and not be a hearer only but a doer of what the Torah says, you shall be blessed in your deeds. You can't be blessed outside of the Torah.

This is why I believe in prosperity, you see. We are going to teach on prosperity. We are going to teach on healing, just like we are going to teach on the works and power of the Holy Spirit.

We want all of the blessings. Let me tell you something. The Almighty is still putting His people above all the people on the earth. He is still doing that. Those of you who have not heard the teaching on *True Biblical Prosperity,* you ought to listen to it. You are going to find that one person's prosperity and another person's prosperity is not the same prosperity.

Think about it, ladies and gentlemen. I think about this all the time. We're going to talk about the widows and the orphans. What greater – I mean, you have a guy over in Dubai who is about to spend twenty billion dollars on a high-rise for luxury so people can go on vacation.

What about having twenty billion dollars to spend on a retirement village? What about a home for the elderly? What about a home for the widows and the orphans? What about a place or a safe haven where these individuals can be? I mean, imagine having that kind of money to spend on luxury items and self.

Now, don't get me wrong, because you will find that even these Torah-observant individuals that are frugal and prudent and cheap; when they go on vacation, they want to sit in front. It bothers me to have to walk past first class to get to coach [on an airplane].

The man of God is sitting in there like a sardine. I'm passing folks. They are sipping on tea and lemonade and wine. The plane doors haven't even shut. The flight attendant is already serving them and has the audacity to close the curtains so you can't see. (Laughter)

I'm sitting back there with the "peasants." Now, don't get me wrong. I'm a man of God! Man, I can't even stretch my legs and don't even let the guy behind me recline! Do you know what? It always seems like they put me in the seat that doesn't recline. I had two flights and I had to change seats. Do you hear me?

The headphones don't work. The seat won't recline. I'm sitting in the middle like this (scrunches up) between two big guys. Meanwhile people are up there in first class sipping lemonade and looking at you as you go by. (Laughter)

How come they get to sit in first class? Who are they? They are not doing what I am doing! They are not saving people's lives! They are not preaching the truth of the Kingdom of the Heavens.

"Well now brother, you better be careful!"

"Yeah."

It's sad that the people of YeHoVaH feel that way about themselves while they believe they serve the King of the Universe. Do you see this? The guy in Dubai is a prince. If we're the sons and daughters of God, then that makes us princes and princesses. How can you take on the mentality of a prince and not take on the mentality of a prince? Do you understand what I am saying?

YeHoVaH didn't put the people of Israel in a 'hood. He didn't put them in a slum. He didn't put them in a ghetto. They caused themselves to end up in a ghetto by violating the commands of YeHoVaH. But YeHoVaH doesn't have a ghetto and a 'hood mentality. He has a mentality where He has a land that is flowing with milk and honey. It has the best resources on the planet!

Do you understand what I am saying? So we have to change our mindset and change our mentality. Let me tell you something. The people of the Kingdom need great wealth. It is going to take great wealth to get this Kingdom message to the ends of the earth! You can't even get on a plane. How are you going to go to the ends of the earth?

But I will tell you who IS going to the ends of the earth. All of these individuals who are preaching another gospel and talking about how:

"We're not under the Law. We're saved by grace."

Now put that into comparison. You will begin to look. Does it look like the church is more prosperous than the Messianic community? They are preaching from the same book! Is it possible that they see some things that we don't see? Or are we too busy pointing the fingers and talking and rejecting the very principles that the Almighty has given us to live by? We've got work to do folks.

> Jas 2:13 – "For he shall have judgment without mercy, that hath shown no mercy; and mercy rejoiceth against judgment."
>
> Jas 2:14 – "What *doth it* profit, my brethren, though a man say he hath faith, and have not works? Can faith save him?"
>
> Jas 2:15 – "If a brother or sister be naked, and destitute of daily food,"

What is he saying? If a brother or sister be naked and destitute of daily food, that means that they have need. It is not just somebody who needs to borrow your coat. They don't have a coat, you see.

> Jas 2:16 – "And one of you say unto them, 'Depart in peace, be *ye* warmed and filled; notwithstanding ye give them not those things which are needful to the body; what *doth it* profit?"
>
> Jas 2:17 – "Even so faith, if it hath not works, is dead, being alone."

You know, if I have two coats and somebody is cold and they don't have one, my role is to give them one of mine. That is what John taught. That is what Yeshua taught.

> Jas 2:18 – "Yea, a man may say, 'Thou hast faith, and I have works: show me thy faith without thy works, and I will show thee my faith by my works."

This is why Martin Luther had a problem with *James*.

> Jas 2:19 – "Thou believest that there is one God; thou doest well: the devils also believe, and tremble."

You see, it is one thing to believe *in* God. It is a whole other thing to *believe* Him. That is what separated Abraham out. Abraham believed and it was counted to him as righteousness. When we believe what the word says, guess what? We do what the word says.

If we say that we believe and we are not doing what it says – if the word says to wear tzitzits and I'm not wearing tzitzits, do I believe what the word says about tzitzits? No, I don't! If the word says tie a ribbon of blue in your tzitzits, why am I wearing all-white ones? Even though I have tzitzits, they are not [true] tzitzits. They are strings. That's all they are. They are strings tied in a knot (Phariseaically).

> Jas 2:20 – "But wilt thou know, O vain man, that faith without works is dead?"

What is he saying? If you've got faith, you're going to see it. You're going to see it. Do you know how a poor person is poor? How do you know a poor person is poor? I mean, you can see poverty. A homeless person – you can see it. A homeless person looks homeless. A prostitute looks like a prostitute. A wealthy person looks like a wealthy person. A poor person looks like a poor person.

Some people are able to hide it. But for the most part, you can see it. You know when you are in a poor neighborhood. You know when you are in a wealthy neighborhood. You can see it. You can see poverty.

> "Why are you talking about poverty and wealth?"

It is because you can see faith. If we watch and look, you can see it. You can hear it. You can hear it in people's conversations. You can hear doubt in people's conversations. You listen. They will tell you where they are.

> Jas 2:21 – "Was not Abraham our father justified by works, when he had offered Isaac his son upon the altar?"

Father says:

> "Take your son, your only son."

He did it.

> Jas 2:22 – "Seest thou how faith wrought with his works, and by works was faith made perfect?"

You see, you can talk about faith all day long. But if your faith doesn't have works, then your faith is in vain. Can you see why Luther, who was teaching "faith alone, you don't need works," said:

> "Not of works brother. No works in this faith."

Well, you can't have faith without works!

> Jas 2:23 – "And the scripture was fulfilled which saith, Abraham believed God, and it

> was imputed unto him for righteousness: and he was called the Friend of God."

Abraham believed. How do you know that he believed? He did what the Almighty told him to do, even though he didn't want to do it. Can you imagine? You have waited your whole life for a child. Now Father says:

> "I want you to kill him."

Imagine that! But Abraham knew this much. He was incapable of having a child by himself. He understood that this child that he had was from the Almighty. And since the Almighty gave him the child, the Almighty had every right to tell him what to do concerning the child. Too many people get things from the Almighty and now the Almighty doesn't have any "say."

> Jas 2:24 – "Ye see then how that by works a man is justified, and not by faith only."

A man is justified by his work. What is he addressing? He is addressing – Paul talks about justification, but Paul doesn't talk about justification apart from work. Many people have interpreted Paul to be an anti-law person. What Paul was anti-law about was not the Law of YeHoVaH, but the law of the Pharisees; of which he used to be one.

The Pharisees didn't keep the Law. They put burdens on people they themselves were not willing to carry.

> Jas 2:25 – "Likewise also was not Rahab the harlot justified by works, when she had received the messengers, and had sent *them* out another way?"

> Jas 2:26 – "For as the body without the spirit is dead, so faith without works is dead also."

Now Martin Luther is reading this stuff, especially after the stuff that he is preaching. He is reading this. He says that *James* should be ripped out of the Bible. *James* does not "belong" in the Bible. That is what he said! This is the Founding Father of the Christian Church, if you would. Folks want to say:

"Well, Paul is the Founding Father."

No, Paul didn't start Christianity. People interpreted Paul. Paul wasn't teaching things that they were saying that Paul taught.

Roman Catholicism and Eastern Orthodoxy argue that this passage disproves the doctrine of justification by faith alone (or *sola fide*). Whereas the early and many modern Protestants continue to believe that Catholic and Orthodox interpretations do not fully understand the meaning of the term "justification" and resolve James' and Paul's apparent conflict regarding faith and works in alternate ways from the Catholics and Orthodox.

Protestants believe that Paul was dealing with one kind of error, while James was dealing with a different error. The errorists that Paul was dealing with were people who said that works of the Law were needed to be added to faith in order to help earn God's favor.

Paul was dealing with this issue. We know that Paul was dealing with this issue. We looked at it. At some point we will look again at *Acts* chapter 15. This was when individuals came to Antioch and were teaching that a person had to first undergo *Brit Milah*, or they had to first be circumcised under the Law of Moses before they could be "saved."

What they were actually teaching was that since faith came to the Jew first, that you had to become a Jew first. They taught that you had to convert to Judaism first before you could be a believer. Every Gentile had to convert to Judaism.

Now, believe it or not, most people today, when they come to the realization that the Christian Church has been teaching them wrongly, they are compelled to begin to look down the path of Judaism and specifically Judaism with a twist of Yeshua.

This is Messianic Judaism. This is why they want to practice these things. You see, Judaism is appealing. Messianic Judaism is appealing to people who want faith in Messiah without going all the way into Judaism. They borrow a lot of Judaism to make it look "authentic." Now you have people looking like Jewish wanna-be's.

This is the biggest statement you hear when you and your family decide that you are going to keep the commandments of YeHoVaH; not the Law of Moses, as it is called. People want to say:

"Okay, you are trying to become Jewish."

Why is it that you are "trying to become Jewish" because you have decided to keep the Law? It is because people have been brainwashed into believing that the Law was only for the Jews. The only people who keep the Law are Jewish. So if you are starting to keep the Law, you must be trying to convert to become a Jew.

Paul counted this error by pointing out that salvation was by faith alone; apart from deeds of the Law. (*Galatians* 2:16; *Romans* 3:21-22).

> Gal 2:16 – "Knowing that a man is not justified by the works of the law, but by the faith **of** Yeshua Messiah,"

I underlined this so that you will see this. So often people read over the word "of." Instead they read "in." He is not saying "in."

> "Knowing that a man is not justified by the works of the law, but by the faith **of** Messiah"

It is not faith "in" Messiah. This is important. This is important. We are going to deal with this as we talk about the true gospel of the kingdom; which I am going to start teaching on this Sabbath. Then as we continue on, we will begin to deal with faith and understanding faith and the many facets of faith as it is taught in the Bible.

> "Knowing that a man is not justified by the works of the law, but by the faith **of** Messiah Yeshua, even we have believed in..."

Do you see this? Those who believe *in* are justified by the faith *of.* There is a difference. It is having *the faith of* Messiah, not just *faith in* Messiah. But if that is not enough:

> "...even we have believed in Yeshua Messiah, that we might be justified by the faith **of** Messiah, and not by the works of the law: for by the woks of the law shall no flesh be justified."

What he is addressing here is that there are some things that the Law and those who teach the Law – guess what? How would people know anything about the Law other than from those who are supposed to be teaching the Law?

What if you have a non-Jewish person who doesn't have access to the scrolls? They don't have the scrolls or the prophets. They don't have any of the writings. All they have is what they see those people do who are supposed to be following the Law.

That is what they see. They don't know the Law. It's just like you have people today. What they know about Christianity is from what they have seen Christians do.

They haven't read the Bible. How can they know about the word of YeHoVaH and they haven't even read the Bible? They've read Christians! That's what they've read.

This happens even with people in church. You go to church and you sit down among the Baptists. You start looking around and observing how people are keeping this Baptist faith. You can't find the Baptist denomination in the Bible. You can't find the Pentecostal denomination in the Bible. A Pentecostal does Pentecostal stuff. A Baptist does Baptist stuff. A Methodist does Methodist stuff. A Catholic does Catholic stuff.

You are practicing your faith. Your faith is what you see other people do. When you are a part of the faith and people are leading people in the faith and you are in the faith and are not doing what other people in the faith are doing, then they now think you are a wolf.

> "Well, wait a minute brother. You've been coming here. You ain't been baptized. You haven't joined the church. You haven't accepted our statement of faith. When other people are up rocking, you are sitting there looking. You never come to the altar looking for prayer."

Do you understand? You don't look like one of them. If you don't look like one of them, you are an odd duck. So to keep from being an odd duck, what do you do? When they stand up, you stand up.

> "Okay, people are standing up. I don't know why I'm standing up, but I'm going to stand up."

Do you know what I am saying? They face the East, you face the East. In some churches, do you know what they do? They don't pass the basket because you can be incognito. They have people get up, go to the altar and put their money in and keep on moving. Now imagine if you don't get up! You've got your little quarter in your hand real tight. You get up and put your hand all the way down into the basket. (Laughs)

You all know what I am talking about. Don't be looking at me like you don't know what I am talking about. I know you "don't." That's because you want to fit in. People want to fit in. They don't want to look odd.

He is talking about the faith of Messiah.

> Gal 2:16 – "for by the works of the law shall no flesh be justified."

We are not trying to get justified by keeping the Law. We are keeping the Law because we have been made righteous.

> Ro 3:20 – "Therefore by the deeds of the law there shall no flesh be justified in his sight: for by the law *is* the knowledge of sin."

> Ro 3:21-22 – "But now the righteousness of God without the law is manifested, being witnessed by the law and the prophets, ²²Even the righteousness of God."

Now Paul – notice here in *Galatians* that he uses this word "of." It is *faith of.* Then he uses the same word in *Romans.*

> Ro 3:22 – "Even the righteousness of God *which is* by faith **of** Messiah Yeshua unto all and upon all them that believe:"

Is that in your Bible too? "Faith of." Now you notice, we don't see that, so I am pointing that out. Why is an "of" such a big issue? It is because what he is saying is that I have to watch what Yeshua did. I have to see what he did.

While I was in California, this was really the message. We learn by two ways. We learn by what we see and we learn by what we hear. Yeshua taught two ways. He taught by what he did and he taught by what he said. The most effective teaching Yeshua did was by what he did.

People weren't drawn to Yeshua because of his message. People were drawn to Yeshua because of what he did. People heard about what he did. They didn't hear about what he preached. They came from miles and miles and miles and miles and miles around. It was because of the works that he did. He said:

> "The works that I do, you shall do, and greater works than these."

When we went to Israel, the issue was, and Father said:

> "Don't go over there trying to preach the Torah. Go and show them faith. Go and show them the work of the Spirit. And in that, you can avoid some of the arguments. But you will notice that when people see the power of the Almighty, they are more apt to listen to what you have to say."

Before that, everybody has an argument. You can't argue with power. This is what they will say, just like Nicodemus.

> "Surely you are one sent from Elohim because no man can do the works you do if Elohim wasn't with you."

So what Father said to me was:

> "You're not going to be another talking head in this Hebrew Roots movement.

You're going to go to the forefront and you're going to show and demonstrate the power of the Almighty. And you are going to call people."

I had folks saying:

"You know, when you first talked about this healing stuff, my walls went up."

I know. So I'm giving people notice months in advance, weeks in advance. You know, they put it out there. Then I had one woman come to me who said:

"I really wanted to come to your message. I wanted to come and hear you teach on the power."

I said:

"Well, where were you?"

"Well, I was over in So-and-So's breakout group."

I said:

"Well, you were where you wanted to be."

Don't come telling me that you wanted to be hearing me. If you wanted to hear me, you would have had your butt sitting in the room where I was teaching. Don't come flattering me with your words. You were where you wanted to be.

"Well, Oo."

You see, I ain't playing! (Laughs) Every now and then I have to smile and laugh to let you know that I ain't mad at you. I ain't mad at you! But don't come shucking and jiving. Don't come playing with the preacher, because I ain't one of that kind. Your words mean nothing. Your actions are what I am watching. You were where your feet took you and your feet took you where you wanted them to take you. Yeah, that will wipe that smile right off of your face.

> Ro 3:22 – "Even the righteousness of God *which is* by faith **of**..."

Not by faith *in* but by faith *of*...

> "...Messiah Yeshua unto all and upon all them that believe: for there is no difference:"

> Ro 3:23 – "For all have sinned, and come short of the glory of God;"

Paul also taught that saving faith is not dead but alive, showing thanks to God in deeds of love (*Galatians* 5:6):

> "For in Messiah Yeshua neither circumcision availeth any thing, nor uncircumcision; but faith which worketh by love.".

So what is he saying? Just because you are circumcised, it doesn't give you a leg up. You can be a circumcised individual without faith. There were a whole bunch of them in the wilderness. Your circumcision doesn't mean anything if you are not operating by faith. A person who is not circumcised but who is operating in faith has the Almighty's attention. It is just like Cornelius. Cornelius was doing some things. YeHoVaH says:

> "I've got to save this man."

He disturbed the apostles. He said:

> "Go to Cornelius' house. He needs to hear the message of faith."

That's because faith cometh by hearing. And while he was listening, the Bible says that the Holy Spirit fell upon his entire house. Imagine that because of Cornelius' faith, everybody in the house – he invited some folks. It wasn't just his family. He invited a whole bunch of people to come and listen to the message. Because of Cornelius' faith, all these people got saved – filled with the Holy Spirit. Imagine your life impacting everybody in your life.

Protestants also believed *James* was dealing with errorists who said that if they had faith, they didn't need to show love by a life of faith. They used *James* 2:14-17. James countered this error by teaching that faith is alive, showing itself to be so by deeds of love (*James* 2:18, 26).

Protestants believe that James and Paul both teach that salvation is by faith alone and also that faith is never alone, but that it shows itself to be alive by deeds of love that express a believer's thanks to God for the free gift of salvation by faith in Yeshua.

Imagine this. This is what people want to talk about.

> "All you have to do is just love, brother. If you love, you fulfill the law."

Really? Do you know what love is? How do you love the kind of love that pleases YeHoVaH? You see, you can do all of the deeds and works, but Yeshua said it very simply:

> "If you love me, you'll keep my commandments."

James says:

> "Here is the love of God, that you keep His commandments."

The way that you demonstrate your love for the Almighty is how? By keeping His commandments. You can do all of these works. You can build and evangelize and do all kinds of miracles. But if you are not keeping the commands, that is all He is really asking you to do.

However, here is the question. Was James addressing errorists as the Protestants teach? What was James dealing with? Who was James? We are going to get into this. Who was James writing to? We have already identified that he was writing to the twelve tribes. The twelve tribes had knowledge of the commandments.

Why was James writing the Book of *James*? James explains it to us. What was James' core message? You see, Martin Luther knew that James was writing to the twelve tribes. Martin Luther also knew that he wasn't one of them. So as far as James is concerned, it was irrelevant.

These individuals back in the day had a different way of approaching the Bible than we do today. It has been so watered down for many people today. It's all about denominationalism. It's not about Bible. It's about what church you go to.

Who was James? The author identifies himself as James in verse one.

> Jas 1:1 – "James, a servant of God and of the Lord Yeshua Messiah,"

He tells us right there who he is writing to.

> "**to the twelve tribes** which are scattered abroad"

> "**to the twelve tribes** which are scattered abroad, greeting."

It was not the Gentiles. It was not the church as we know of that is full of Gentiles. It was not the Jews. James is very clear. He doesn't need anybody to interpret what he is saying. He has made it very clear that he is writing to the twelve tribes which are scattered abroad. James knows some things. Do you know what? James is part of that tribe.

James' core message is a message of faith. It is a message of faith. He makes it very clear early on. He is talking about faith throughout his message. In chapter one he is talking about faith. In chapter two he is talking about faith. Even when he gets to chapter five he talks about the prayer of faith.

He is calling the elders if there are any sick. James teaches us about some faith and encouraging people in their faith even though they have been scattered abroad. They have been chased out of town. They have been run out of the homeland. Keep your faith! No matter where you go and what you do, keep your faith! We're going to see this in a little detail.

It was believed that James was one of the brothers of Yeshua and probably the oldest.

> Mt 13:55 – "Isn't this the carpenter's son? Isn't his mother's name Mary, and aren't his brothers James, Joseph, Simon and Judas?"

Now this Judas here is believed to have written the Book of *Jude.* James is believed to have written the Book of *James.* Neither of them were believers while Yeshua was alive. I will leave you with that.

You have learned about hermeneutics. You've learned about the principles. Wouldn't it be nice to just walk through a book and really just pull out of it what is really there? That is what you should do with every book of the Bible; every last one of them from *Genesis* to *Revelation.*

It is very difficult to start in the middle of a book and then to understand what the writer is trying to communicate. You just can't do it. But because somebody decided that they would break the books down into chapters and verses, now you can start at any chapter and at any verse and start a conversation out of context to make a point and to preach a doctrine. Hallelujah. ∎

Shalom!

You have just enjoyed one of the many fine teachings available through Arthur Bailey Ministries. Our full selection of teachings are available at:

www.ArthurBaileyMinistries.com

Are you interested in learning more about the *True Gospel* and how to better communicate the word of YeHoVaH? Here at Arthur Bailey Ministries, we now offer the world's first Messianic, Hebrew Roots of the Faith, **Discipleship Training Program.** This exclusive learning opportunity is available in workbook and DVD formats and also online here for individual or classroom study:

www.discipleship101.tv

Thank you for your interest in our products and ministry teachings! We invite you to participate in our fellowship services at House Of Israel in Charlotte; through one of our satellite locations, or via the Internet. Please see our web site for our weekly television broadcast schedule and live internet events. We are reaching, preaching, and teaching the *True Gospel of the Kingdom of YeHoVaH to the Whole World.* **We would be honored if you would join us!**

Fellowship Location
House Of Israel
1334 Hill Road
Charlotte, NC 28210

Mailing Address
Arthur Bailey Ministries
PO Box 49744
Charlotte, NC 28277

Office Phone
888-899-1479

Join us each week for our LIVE broadcasts
Thursdays @ 7pm ET • Saturdays @ 11am ET

Taking the True Gospel
of the Kingdom of YeHoVaH
to the Whole World.

DVD Teachings By Arthur Bailey

In this 4-DVD teaching, Arthur Bailey expounds on each blessing; summarizes the 28 Blessings of *Deuteronomy 28,* and identifies what these blessings look like in our day and time. You will learn how these blessings manifest, and the importance of living a Torah Observant Spirit-Filled Life in order to experience the fullness of the "The 28 Blessings of Deuteronomy 28."
Approximately 5 hrs.

28 Blessings of Deuteronomy 28   4 DVDs – $45.00

In this exciting teaching you will learn what are considered to be the Firstfruits Offerings; when they are to be presented, and why Firstfruits Offerings are so important! You will also learn the prayer that is recited during this vital offering which assures the blessing of prosperity upon those who present this offering unto YeHoVaH.
Approximately 1.5 hrs.

Feast of Firstfruits
1 DVD – $15.00

DVD Teachings By Arthur Bailey

"Hear, O Israel" is a call for ALL of the People Of YeHoVaH to Hear and to Obey His Commands. Often times when people hear the word "Israel," they think "Jews." Israel consists of 12 Tribes; the Jews are only one of those tribes. In this eye-opening, engaging and life-changing teaching "Hear, O Israel," Arthur Bailey explains in-depth of Yeshua's response and the benefits of what it really means to Hear and to Obey! Approximately 2.5 hrs.

Hear, O Israel   2 DVDs – $25.00

In this dynamic, life-changing teaching: "How To Hear God's Voice," author and teacher Arthur Bailey shares important Biblical truths that will help you identify and distinguish the voice of the Almighty from all other voices. In this 4-DVD collection you will learn:
- Why YeHoVaH communicates with His people
- Why he wants you to hear His voice
- How to identify His voice from others
- Where he most likely speaks to you

And so much more! Approximately 5.5 hrs.

How To Hear God's Voice   4 DVDs – $45.00

DVD Teachings By Arthur Bailey

In this 2-DVD teaching series, Arthur Bailey presents from Scripture how the relationships in our lives must be categorized and prioritized according to their importance. You will learn:

- The kind of relationship the Almighty wants with you
- How to categorize and prioritize your relationships according to Scripture
- How to identify and rectify wrong relationships

And so much more! Approximately 2.5 hrs.

Relationships   2 DVDs – $25.00

Join Arthur Bailey as he explains the parable taught by Yeshua after having shared with His disciples about the Gospel of The Kingdom being preached to the whole world before the end comes. Yeshua gives a parable about three servants who were given specific talents. What distinguished the wise servant from the wicked servant in this parable was determined by what they did with the talents they had been given. Approximately 1.5 hrs.

Maximizing Your Talents   1 DVD – $15.00

DVD Teachings By Arthur Bailey

Where did Christmas originate? What does the Bible have to say about Christmas and its relationship to the birth of Christ? Is Christmas even in the Bible? Should Christ be in Christmas? Is Jesus the reason for the season? How should true believers respond to Christmas? These questions and so many more will be answered in this timeless Christmas Message, "MERRY CHRISTMAS?"
Approx. 1.5 hrs.

Merry Christmas?   1 DVD – $15.00

The ReNEWed Covenant is 1.5 hours of teaching. In this teaching "The ReNEWed Covenant," Arthur Bailey gives a clear, eye-opening, biblical explanation of what the New Covenant is, and with whom it is made. He explains how Jews and Gentiles enter into this covenant, and what it means for believers today. You will understand why it is called The ReNEWed Covenant, and the significant power that is released within the lives of all who embrace the ReNEWed Covenant. This Teaching Will Change Your Life Forever! Approximately 1.5 hrs.

The ReNEWed Covenant   1 DVD – $15.00

DVD Teachings By Arthur Bailey

In this powerful 4-DVD teaching "The Power of The Holy Spirit," author and teacher Arthur Bailey reveals the pre-requisites all believers must meet to be filled with the Holy Spirit and Power. What is this power Yeshua spoke of? Is this power still available for the disciples of Yeshua today? How can the disciples of Yeshua operate in this power today? These and many other questions will be answered in this fascinating and informative teaching series. Approximately 5.5 hrs.

The Power of the Holy Spirit   4 DVDs – $45.00

In this teaching Arthur Bailey will address:

- What is Prosperity?
- Is Prosperity Biblical?
- Is Poverty a Curse?
- Can Believers be Prosperous?
- What does the Bible Teach about Prosperity?
- What is True Biblical Prosperity?

What you believe about prosperity will determine what you can and cannot receive from YeHoVaH. This teaching series will leave you with a wealth of information. It will help you understand why YeHoVaH wants His people to be *prosperous*, and what *true Biblical prosperity* looks like! Approximately 5.5 hrs.

True Biblical Prosperity   4 DVDs – $45.00

DVD Teachings By Arthur Bailey

The Church world has taken a conversation Yeshua had with a Pharisee at night, and built powerhouse ministries teaching a gospel message of salvation and altar calls. Many sermons have been taught about being born again and what it should mean to believers today. But what does *John 3:16* really teach us within the context it is written? Like many other Biblical passages, this much-quoted verse is taught and preached in a manner that has become isolated from the passage context in which it was originally written. Approximately 2.5 hrs.

You Must Be Born Again   2 DVDs – $25.00

Paul wrote in the book of Romans, *"But God commendeth his love toward us, in that, while we were yet sinners, Messiah died for us"*. God demonstrated His love for us by giving His only begotten Son to die for our sins. How can we show our love for God? In this 4-DVD teaching, Arthur Bailey will take you on a journey through the *greatest love story ever written*, and what our response to the love of God should be. It is more than just a story of salvation. It is a story of love; of overcoming, of victory, and of power. Approx. 5.5 hrs.

The Love of God   4 DVDs – $45.00

DVD Teachings By Arthur Bailey

The Fall Feasts of YeHoVaH is a 6-DVD set with over 6.5 hours of teaching. This series include teachings on The Feast of Trumpets/Yom Teruah, Day of Atonement/Yom Kippur, The Feast of Tabernacles/Sukkot and The Last Great Day/Shemini Atzeret. The Introduction to the Fall Feasts will not only provide insight and understanding of the prophetic shadow pictures of good things to come; it will also help us understand how to celebrate these amazing days in a way that pleases Almighty YeHoVaH.

The Fall Feasts Of YeHoVaH   6 DVDs – $65.00

Now Concerning Spiritual Gifts is a 6-DVD set with over 6.5 hours of teaching. Many suggest that the gifts of the Spirit have ceased to be in operation, just as they also insist that the Law is done away with. Among those who accept and teach that the spiritual gifts of the Bible are still operational today, many have abused and misused these gifts in their assembly; similar to those in the days of the Corinthian assembly Paul wrote to correct — thus the controversy! In this series, Arthur Bailey takes the mystery out of manifesting spiritual gifts and empowers believers.

Now Concerning Spiritual Gifts   6 DVDs – $65.00

DVD Teachings By Arthur Bailey

The New Covenant — When did the New Covenant begin? Join Arthur Bailey as he journeys inside the first Jerusalem Council as the Apostles, Elders and Ruach Ha Kodesh discuss how to deal with a false teaching that was circulating among believers. Arthur Bailey is a spirit-filled, New Covenant minister who boldly teaches the Hebrew Roots of the Christian faith and takes the confusion out of covenants that are as important today as they were long ago. Includes two episodes.

The New Covenant   1 DVD – $15.00

Keeping Torah Living Spirit Filled. Join Arthur Bailey as he journeys inside the first Jerusalem Council as the Apostles, Elders and Ruach Ha Kodesh discuss how to deal with a false teaching that was circulating among the believers and how to incorporate the Gentile converts into the newly formed Messianic community. This teaching will deepen your understanding of the early Hebrew culture and strengthen your walk in Yeshua Messiah. Three episodes. About 1.5 hours of teaching.

Keeping Torah Living Spirit Filled   1 DVD – $15.00

DVD Teachings By Arthur Bailey

The Baptism of the Holy Spirit — Yeshua said in Acts 1 verse 5: *"For John truly baptized with water; but ye shall be baptized with the Holy Ghost not many days hence."* And in verse 8: *"But ye shall receive power, after that the Holy Ghost is come upon you: and ye shall be witnesses unto me both in Jerusalem, and in all Judea, and in Samaria, and unto the uttermost parts of the earth."*

When we are baptized with the Holy Spirit, we receive power and authority not just to speak for YeHoVaH, but to demonstrate His power! In this 4-DVD teaching series, you will learn what is the true evidence of the baptism of the Holy Spirit and so much more! A must-have for every true believer who wants to walk in their authority. Over 5 hours of teaching!

The Baptism of the Holy Spirit   4 DVDs – $45.00

Walking in the Power of the Holy Spirit; My Testimony. Join Arthur Bailey as he shares experiences and unique insights in this perceptive, sometimes hilarious and always instructive journey through his ministry spanning more than three decades. He generously shares his life-changing adventures of discovering and tapping back into the roots of the faith that he has long preached with boldness. As a former pastor and teacher in five different Christian denominations before coming to the true faith of the Kingdom of YeHoVaH, his unique story is priceless and required listening for those who desire to enhance their own walk in Torah-obedience and in Yeshua Messiah. About 1.5 hours of teaching.

Walking in the Power of the Holy Spirit; My Testimony
1 DVD – $20.00

DVD Teachings By Arthur Bailey

And The Heavens Were Opened. In this 3 DVD series, Arthur Bailey takes you on an in-depth, inspiring journey through Shavuot, Yom Teruah and Hanukkah to reveal the importance of these biblical events for today's Spirit-filled believer in Yeshua. Learn more about operating in the gifts of the Holy Spirit, the works of Yeshua Messiah and the re-dedication of the second temple at Hanukkah. About 4.5 hours of teaching.

And The Heavens Were Opened   3 DVDs – $35.00

And You Shall Love The Lord... The Creator of the Universe demonstrated His love for us by sacrificing His only begotten Son for the sins of man. The Love of God is a gift! You can-not earn it. You do not deserve it. You cannot buy it. So how do we demonstrate our love for God? Often when sharing the Gospel of Yeshua (the Gospel <u>Yeshua taught</u> *not* the Gospel <u>about Jesus</u>), the subject of the "Law" comes up. Yeshua clearly stated that he did not come to do away with or to abolish the Law (Matthew 5:17). Yet people still argue that we must only "love" YeHoVaH with all of our heart, mind, soul and strength. Are we doing that? What does loving God look like? The Bible instructs us how YeHoVaH wants us to show our love for Him. Learn the truth and find answers to many questions you won't learn from religion. About 2.5 hours of teaching.

And You Shall Love The Lord...   2 DVDs – $25.00

DVD Teachings By Arthur Bailey

In this 2 DVD set, learn about how according to Acts 15, a major challenge existed which con-fronted the newly formed Messianic community. Arthur Bailey journeys in-side the first Jerusalem Council where the Apostles, Elders and the Ruach Ha Kodesh discussed how to deal with a false teaching that was circulating among the early believers and how to incorporate Gentile converts into the newly formed Messianic community. Many traditional Jewish believers in Yeshua struggled with how to go from a totally ethnic Jewish religious community to one which included non-Hebrew people who were unfamiliar with the rich heritage and traditions formed by the Pharisees and handed down by the Elders. This teaching will deepen and strengthen your spiritual walk in Yeshua Messiah as you learn more about the history of the early called-out ones of faith. 2 episodes.

What Do We Do With Those Gentiles?   1 DVD – $15.00

Today there is as much confusion about being "Messianic" as there is on certain issues across denominational Christianity. As more and more people's eyes are opened to the faith once delivered to the saints and new believers are being added to the family of YeHoVaH, it is vitally important that they get started on the path the right way. In this very important teaching, Arthur Bailey shares what every new believer must know to live a power-filled, successful life in the Kingdom of YeHoVaH. You will learn who you are in Messiah, the importance of the faith, the baptism of the Holy Spirit, how to properly respond to the Sabbath argument, the dietary laws and feast days and much more. About 2 hours of teaching.

Messianic 101: "The Essentials"   2 DVDs – $25.00

The DVDs listed in this book are just a sampling of the many teachings produced by Arthur Bailey Ministries. The teaching DVDs are packed with scriptural references and are taught in a format that will encourage, strengthen and enhance your spiritual journey to help you grow to maturity in Messiah Yeshua.

We invite you to enroll in our Discipleship Training Program, the only true Messianic Hebrew Roots of the faith Discipleship program on the planet! Learn the real history of the faith once delivered to the saints and prepare yourself for biblical discussions, ministry services and/or ordination. This comprehensive program is at a collegiate level yet written for all believers to understand, no matter where they are in their walk.

This series of 105 classes may be viewed *FREE* online. There are also informative workbooks available for purchase that are designed to accompany the two-year Discipleship course. Visit the Discipleship Training Program web site at:

Discipleship101.tv

Feel free to visit our ministry web site to order any of our DVDs, books and other teaching materials and supplies through the ministry's online store.

www.ArthurBaileyMinistries.com/Bookstore

In addition to our broadcast television teachings, we also have a dedicated web site called SpiritFilledLiving.tv where you can conveniently watch any number of our fine teachings.

Our video teachings also appear on our YouTube Channel.
Please subscribe to our free Newsletter.

You may place your order online on our secure website, phone in your order at 1-888-899-1479, or send your check or money order to:

Arthur Bailey Ministries
P.O. Box 49744
Charlotte, NC 28277

Your Support is Highly Appreciated.
Be Blessed in Yeshua Messiah! Shalom!

Made in the USA
Middletown, DE
21 July 2023